Egyptian Pyramids Revisited

Expanded Third Edition

Moustafa Gadalla

Tehuti Research Foundation
International Head Office: Greensboro, NC, U.S.A.

Egyptian Pyramid Revisited – Expanded Third Edition
by MOUSTAFA GADALLA

Published by:

Tehuti Research Foundation
P.O. Box 39491
Greensboro, NC 27438, U.S.A.

This book is a revised and enhanced third edition of the second edition entitled: Pyramid Handbook; which was an update of the first edition: *Pyramid Illusions: A Journey to the Truth*, by Moustafa Gadalla. The name was changed to better reflect the content of the book, and to avoid the appearance of self-righteousness.

First ed. issued in 1997 under title Pyramid illusions—ISBN 0-9652509-7-0
Second ed. issued 2000 in paperback—ISBN: 0-9652509-4-6 and 2003 in eBook—ISBN: 1-931446-11-3

Publisher's Cataloging-in-Publication

Gadalla, Moustafa, 1944-
Egyptian Pyramids Revisited / by Moustafa Gadalla
. — 3rd ed., rev.
p. cm.
Includes bibliographical references.
LCCN: 2016900019

ISBN-13(pdf): 978-1-931446-79-2

ISBN-13(e-book): 978-1-931446-80-8
ISBN-13(pbk.): 978-1-931446-81-5

1. Pyramids—Egypt. 2. Egypt—Antiquities. 3. Geometry—Philosophy.
4. Stone, Cast. 5. Masonry—Egypt—History. I. Gadalla, Moustafa,
1944- Egyptian Pyramids Revisited. II. Title.

DT63.G24 2016   932

Updated 2018

CONTENTS

ABOUT THE AUTHOR

Moustafa Gadalla is an Egyptian-American independent Egyptologist who was born in Cairo, Egypt in 1944. He holds a Bachelor of Science degree in civil engineering from Cairo University.

Gadalla is the author of twenty two published internationally acclaimed books about the various aspects of the Ancient Egyptian history and civilization and its influences worldwide.

He is the Founder and Chairman of the Tehuti Research Foundation (**https://www.egypt-tehuti.org**), an international, U.S.-based, non-profit organization dedicated to Ancient Egyptian studies. He is also the Founder and Head of the online Egyptian Mystical University (**https://www.EgyptianMysticalUniversity.org**).

From his early childhood, Gadalla pursued his Ancient Egyptian roots with passion, through continuous study and research. Since 1990, he has dedicated and concentrated all his time to researching and writing.

PREFACE

From a distance, what we have learned about the pyramids may appear factual; but once we examine this information closer, it proves to be otherwise. This book is intended to undo many false perceptions about the Ancient Egyptians' pyramids.

This book provides a fresh look at the interiors and exteriors of Egypt's masonry pyramids, theories of construction, their purpose and function, and the sacred geometry of their design.

This book is a revised and enhanced third edition of the second edition (entitled *Pyramid Handbook*) which was an update of the first edition, *Pyramid Illusions: A Journey to the Truth*, by Moustafa Gadalla.

It should be noted that the digital edition of this book as published in PDF and E-book formats have a substantial number of photographs that compliment the text materials throughout the book.

This expanded edition of the book consists of seven fully illustrated parts, with a total of 18 chapters.

Part I: Overview consists of two chapters—1 and 2, as follows:

Chapter 1: **The Background** provides a short opening statement about the common "theories" and the counterpoints, based on actual facts.

Chapter 2: **The Genuine Masonry Pyramids** provides a list of the Egyptian pyramids that were built during the Fourth dynasty about 4,500 years ago.

Part II: Pyramids versus Tombs consists of two chapters—3 and 4—as follows:

Chapter 3: **Stepped "Pyramid" of Zoser** covers details of its super-structure and its underground chambers.

Chapter 4: **The Fictional Tombs** covers the details of a typical Ancient Egyptian tomb and how totally different it is from the interiors of the Egyptian masonry pyramids of the Fourth Dynasty.

Part III: Pyramids—Functions & Forms consists of two chapters—5 and 6—as follows:

Chapter 5: **The Pyramid Complex** shows how the Egyptian pyramid was a component of a complex that was connected to other temples; and the differences in functions and forms between a pyramid and a temple; as well as the energetic proportioning of such structures.

Chapter 6: **Pyramid Power** covers the form variations of the Egyptian masonry pyramids; and how such forms attract, maintain and channel cosmic energies.

Part IV: Pyramid Construction Techniques consists of two chapters—7 and 8—as follows:

Chapter 7: **The Flawed "Common Theory"** covers the details of the Common 'Theory"; the unidentified "source" of quarried blocks; the impossibilities of cutting and shaping the pyramid blocks; the impossible logistics of the fabricated ramps theory; the conveniently-ignored three immense Pyramids of Snefru; and a summation refuting the western-made "Common Theory".

Chapter 8: **The Material Facts** covers Herodotus' accounts of pyramid construction; Egyptian molding techniques; the differences between synthetic and natural blocks; the various types of synthetic concrete blocks; the unique qualities of the pyramids' casing stones; and additional evidential facts of synthetic pyramid blocks; as well as bringing to light the even more outstanding details of the earlier incredible masonry works of Saqqara.

Part V: The Three Snefru Pyramids consists of three chapters—9 through 11—as follows:

Chapter 9: **Snefru's Meidum Pyramid** covers its detailed exteriors and interiors.

Chapter 10: **Snefru's Bent Pyramid** covers its detailed exteriors and interiors.

Chapter 11: **Snefru's Red Pyramid** covers its detailed exteriors and interiors.

Part VI: The Three Pyramids of Giza consists of four chapters—12 through 15—as follows:

Chapter 12: **The Giza Plateau** provides an overall diagram of the main points of interest in the Giza Plateau.

Chapter 13: **Khufu's Great Pyramid** covers its detailed exteriors and interiors.

Chapter 14: **Khafra's Pyramid** covers its detailed exteriors and interiors.

Chapter 15: **Menkaura's Pyramid** covers its detailed exteriors and interiors.

Part VII: After The Pyramids consists three chapters—16 through 18—as follows:

Chapter 16: **Mission Accomplished** concludes the Egyptians' objectives of building the pyramids.

Chapter 17: **"Pyramid" Texts** covers the origin of such incorrectly Western characterization of such texts.

Chapter 18: **The Greatest Pharaohs That Followed** provides accounts of subsequent, more powerful, and great builders who never built a pyramid because the real objectives of building pyramids were achieved during the era of the Fourth dynasty.

Join us on our journey to find the truth—the WHOLE truth—about the pyramids.

Read this book as an unbiased, fair juror.

Moustafa Gadalla

MAP OF ANCIENT EGYPT

PART I.

OVERVIEW

CHAPTER 1.

THE BACKGROUND

We were taught in school that the pyramids are nothing but tombs which were built by tyrant Pharaohs, and that slaves were used to haul these big stones up temporary ramps in the construction of these pyramids. These commonly held views are without any evidence.

When one examines the facts, especially as one visits the pyramids, one will find that commonly-held beliefs about the pyramids are so incredibly illogical that you may doubt yourself.

The presented evidence in this book will prove the falsehoods of the existing, yet unfounded, formulated 'theories'.

In this book, exhaustive evidence is provided to show that:

1. The stone pyramids are NOT tombs.

2. The stone blocks were man-made and could never have been quarried.

CHAPTER 2.

THE GENUINE MASONRY PYRAMIDS

There are numerous structures which have/had a real or the apparent shape of a pyramid. The genuine pyramids, however, are those which consist of solid-core masonry. People forget that a pyramid by geometric definition (as they studied in school) is "a solid figure having a polygonal base, the sides of which form the bases of triangular surfaces meeting at a common vertex".

These masonry Egyptian pyramids were all built during the 4th Dynasties. In a little more than a century, 25 million tons of limestone was used to build these pyramids. Later, ungenuine "pyramids" were built during the 5th and later Dynasties.

The ungenuine "pyramids" are built of loose stone rubble and sand—basically, the refuse site's excavated material—piled and sandwiched between stone walls. Most are now little more than heaps of rubble, because this type of construction rapidly deteriorates once the casing is badly damaged or removed.

As for the main Egyptian masonry pyramids of the

Fourth Dynasty, they are, in the order that they were built:

1. The Meidum Pyramid during the reign of Snefru—2575-2551 BCE

2. The Bent Pyramid at Dahshur during the reign of Snefru—2575-2551 BCE

3. The Red Pyramid at Dahshur during the reign of Snefru—2575-2551 BCE

4. The Giza Pyramid of Khufu (Cheops)—2551-2528 BCE

5. The Giza Pyramid of Khafra (Chephren)—2520-2494 BCE

6. The Giza Pyramid of Menkaura (Mycerinus)—2494-2472 BCE

The commonly labeled Step "Pyramid" in Saqqara is not a pyramid per the usual definition (as well other reasons that will be detailed in the next chapter).

The true pyramids of the Fourth Dynasty are totally void of ANY religious inscription. They have been attributed to specific Pharaohs, based on Herodotus' accounts and references that indirectly refer to these Pharaohs' names on some nearby buildings and tombs.

One should conclude that these were unselfish kings who built them for a higher and nobler cause, and not as personal monuments.

There was definitely a master plan that required this particular number of pyramids, with their specific sizes and configurations, at specific locations.

PART II.

PYRAMIDS VERSUS
TOMBS

CHAPTER 3.

STEPPED "PYRAMID" OF ZOSER

3.1 THE SUPER-STRUCTURE

There are main facts about the super-structure that was built by Zoser:

(1) It is not really a pyramid

(2) The final shape of the structure consisting of stepped stone layers was never the original intent of the structure.

The original objective was to build a mastaba-type tomb in which to bury the king when he died. Building a step "pyramid" was an afterthought that occurred a few years later.

The mastaba-type tomb is functionally and structurally independent of the later addition of the stepped "pyramid".

The transformation from an original mastaba-type tomb to a Step Pyramid occurred over five stages of construction.

The stages of construction can be followed because almost all the outer casing has disappeared, as well as many layers of the core masonry. The eastern, southern, and northern faces show clearly the five distinct construction stages.

The five construction stages are:

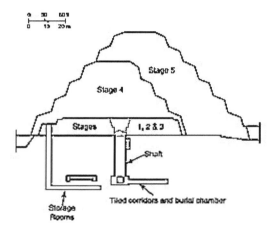

The first stage was the building of an unusual square stone mastaba 120 x 120 x 15 cubits (206' x 206' x 26') [63 m x 63 m x 8 m] (others were rectangular), with an underground burial chamber. The core masonry was made of small stone blocks, laid like bricks. The stone mastaba was faced with fine limestone, which proves it was intended to be a finished building.

The second stage comprised the addition of 6 cubits (10', 3 m) of fine limestone around the perimeter of the mastaba.

The third stage was the addition of a further 15 cubits (25', 7.5 m) extension to the eastern face, providing a rectangular ground plan. An additional central shaft, a series of corridors and another tomb chamber were also dug.

The fourth stage was the construction of a four-tiered structure of stone, weighing 200,000 tons, on top of the existing tomb structure.

The fifth stage was the addition of two more steps and the final six-tiered pyramid, was, in turn, faced with fine limestone to give it a smooth finish.

Final Dimensions:

> Height: 115 cubits (197' or 60m)
> Base: 270 x 225 cubits (459' x 387' or 140m x 118m)

In simple terms, this structure is basically a mastaba-type tomb which was covered with a series of limestone steps.

>> The main purpose of this structure was the burial of Zoser and his family. The Step Pyramid was an afterthought.

>> The burial chambers are not an integral part of the pyramid structure.

3.2 UNDERGROUND CHAMBERS

The underground chambers underneath the step structure are vastly different than the steep and restrictive passages in the true pyramids of Giza, Dahshur and Meidum.

In Saqqara, at the bottom of the shaft, there are the burial chambers and a network of passages and small chambers, used for storing the funerary equipment and for the burials of Zoser and five members of his family.

The burial chambers of this stepped structure are burial chambers beyond any doubt. They contain inscriptions, offering rooms, and most of the other funerary features found in both earlier and later tombs. Some of these underground chambers are lined with beautiful blue faience tiles.

There are those who want to credit the invention of blue faience tiles to others in Europe. They claim, without any proof, that the walls were lined with these tiles much later than Zoser's time.

Their claim is groundless. The so-called "Southern Tomb" [see map of Zoser Complex later on], just 700′ (210 m) from the Step "Pyramid" and which was built during Zoser's reign, is lined with the very same tiles. The "Southern Tomb" was intact until it was discovered by the Egyptologists Lauer and Firth in 1924–26.

• • •

It is here, in some of these underground rooms, that the 40,000 items—including stone jars and vessels of every imaginable size, shape, and material—were found.

• • •

The Ancient Egyptian typical tomb consists of two parts:

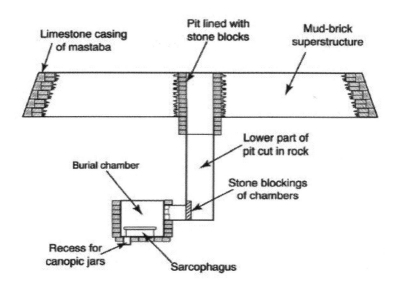

A Cross-Section of a Typical Mastaba-Type Tomb

The superstructures were rectangular, low in proportion to their lengths, and with convex roofs. They varied in size from 24 sq. yards. (20 sq. m) to an area of more than ¼ acre.

The subterranean parts contained the burial chambers, which were surrounded by many other chambers and store rooms for the less important funerary goods. The burial chamber was a narrow chamber hewn out of the rock, to which a shaft leds down from the roof of the mastaba.

>>> Several photographs in support of the text of this chapter are to be found in the digital edition of this book as published in PDF and E-book formats.

CHAPTER 4.

THE FICTIONAL TOMBS

We were taught in school that the pyramids are nothing but tombs.

When we examine the facts of the pyramids, you will find that all these commonly-held beliefs about them are so incredibly baseless that your faith in your education and background may be shattered.

Practically all film and television documentaries about pyramids show outside views of the pyramids,followed by the interior of Tutankhamen's tomb, which was built 2,000 years after the pyramids and is located hundreds of miles from the pyramids!

The deception is clear, since the narrow and plain interiors of the Egyptian pyramids [as shown below] are vastly different than the spacious, richly decorated interiors of Egyptian tombs!

When we look at the Giza Plateau, we see that the Giza pyramids are surrounded by hundreds of tombs commonly known as mastabas. These are the true burial places of the Egyptians, where kings were buried (among other people) before and after the construction of the pyramids.

One must understand Egyptian burial customs. The kings were buried in simple rectangular wooden chests covered with funerary texts and inscriptions. The wooden coffin was placed inside a stone sarcophagus, which was also covered with funerary texts and inscriptions.

>> The vital significance of the sacred inscription in the Egyptian tomb can never be overemphasized. For Egyptians, these inscriptions acted as reference guides or maps for the individual to find her/his way through the afterlife. The symbolic and representative figures and sculptures and implements were intended to meet whatever needs the individual had in that afterlife.

The great masonry pyramids in Giza, Dahshur, and Meidum are totally devoid of these most important sacred inscriptions.

— —

The following are the major differences between the pyramids and Egyptian tombs:

▲ Firstly, these true-shaped pyramids are totally devoid of ANY religious inscriptions, offering rooms, and other funerary features found in both earlier and later tombs. The lack of these items, alone, invalidates its function as a tomb, because funerary rites were essential for the deceased's journey in the beyond.

The sacred inscriptions acted as reference guides or maps

for the individual to find her/his way through the after-world, while the symbolic and representative figures and sculptures and implements were intended to meet whatever needs the individual had in the afterlife.

▲ Secondly, there are too few empty "stone chests" and too many empty rooms in these true-shaped pyramids, to theorize that they were tombs.

▲ Thirdly, if we accept, hypothetically, that robbers might have smashed the stone chests and their lids, one can hardly accept the logic that these robbers would have taken the trouble to steal the smashed stone chests. In spite of careful search, no chips of broken stone chests or their lids were found anywhere in the pyramids' passages and chambers.

▲ Fourthly, the passageways in the true-shaped pyramids are too narrow to provide for the manipulation of stone chests. These true-shaped pyramids are clearly lacking adequate space arrangements for both people and manipulating ceremonial objects.

We know from examinations of numerous mummies from the Pyramid Age Era that people were taller than five feet (1.5 m), which makes these passages [less than 4 feet (1.2 m) high] impossible to walk upright.

We see such restricted passages in all the great Egyptian masonry pyramids, as shown earlier, which will be detailed in each pyramid, later on.

Compare the narrow steep passages in the masonry pyramids with any Egyptian tomb. We find that the Egyptian tombs have spacious passageways for people and for manipulating ceremonial objects.

▲ Fifthly, one Pharaoh, Snefru (2575-2551 BCE), built three pyramids; and nobody expects him to be buried in all three of them.

▲ Lastly, no human remains were ever found inside the nine masonry pyramids. Thieves steal treasures, but they would, naturally, avoid dead bodies.

As you review the sites and interiors of these true-shaped pyramids, you will discover the overwhelming evidence that the pyramids were not built to entomb anybody.

>>> Several photographs in support of the text of this chapter are to be found in the digital edition of this book as published in PDF and E-book formats.

PART III.

PYRAMIDS—FUNCTIONS & FORMS

CHAPTER 5.

THE PYRAMID COMPLEX

5.1 PYRAMIDS AND TEMPLES

It is incorrect to view the pyramid as an independent unit. We must view the pyramid as a component of a multi-component complex, which was the case with all true masonry pyramids of the 4th Dynasty. Each of these real pyramids was a part of a classical pyramid complex [shown below] that consisted of a pyramid and its pyramid temple (erroneously known as *mortuary temple*), with a causeway to a valley temple at the river's bank.

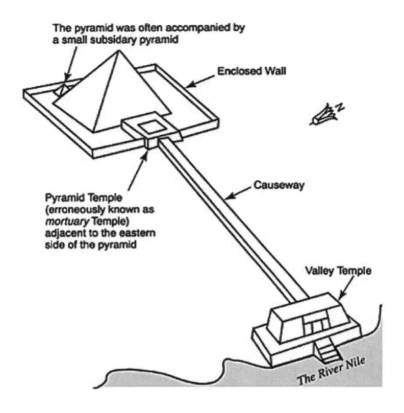

The pyramid was often accompanied by a small subsidary pyramid

Enclosed Wall

Pyramid Temple (erroneously known as *mortuary* Temple) adjacent to the eastern side of the pyramid

Causeway

Valley Temple

The River Nile

The TRUE pyramids were closed and sealed structures. The pyramids were not open for daily activities/rituals, which were performed in the two associated temples within the pyramid complex.

A surviving example in the Giza Plateau is the Khafra Pyramid Complex.

5.2 THE ENERGETIC PROPORTIONING OF THE PYRAMID TEMPLE

As we have shown before, each true pyramid was a part of

a pyramid complex. The pyramid was sealed and inaccessible, with no inscriptions or depictions. Ritual activities took place in the temples next to these pyramids.

It is easy to establish the locations of the various walls of this pyramid temple. We can see from this schematic that this temple was designed to conform to the Summation Series thousands of years before its wrong accreditation to Fibonacci as in the "Fibonacci Series". (The series goes 2, 3, 5, 8, 13, 21, etc.)

The Khafra pyramid temple [shown below] follows TEN consecutive numbers of this series.

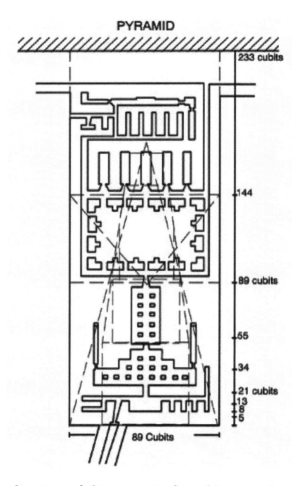

PYRAMID

233 cubits

144

89 cubits

55

34

21 cubits
13
8
5

89 Cubits

The application of this series is found in countless structures throughout the history of Ancient Egypt.

The summation series is reflected throughout nature. It is the natural law that governs growth throughout our universe.

The Egyptians understood the cosmic laws of nature, and all their actions conformed to such laws. They harmonized with nature because man is a part of nature.

The Ancient Egyptians designed their works according to a very strict canon of proportion. The evidence of this detailed canon and its application is overwhelming throughout the history of Ancient Egypt. Using the principles of sacred geometry, the Golden Section [commonly known as Phi] and the circle index [commonly known as Pi], as well as the Summation Series [so-called Fibonacci Series], appears more than 5,000 years ago in all aspects of its architecture, both in whole and in part. [For more information, see the book, The *Ancient Egyptian Mystical Architecture* by Moustafa Gadalla.]

>>> Several photographs in support of the text of this chapter are to be found in the digital edition of this book as published in PDF and E-book formats.

CHAPTER 6.

PYRAMID POWER

6.1 FORM VARIATIONS OF PYRAMIDS

The relationship between process and structure—or function and form – applies to a pyramid with its harmonic design configuration.

The pyramid shape consists of a square base and triangle volume.

- The Ancient Egyptian framework was usually a square, representing the manifested world (i.e. squaring of the circle).

- Egyptians utilized different forms of triangles in their designs, depending on the function/objective of each.

Numerous Egyptian amulets representing the mason's level have been discovered and are now scattered throughout the museums of the world (Turin, Louvre, etc.). The 5:8 triangle represents the greatest percentage of these shapes, which also included the 3:4:5 right-angle triangle and the equilateral triangle

Δ   Δ   Δ

People love to look at the majestic Egyptian pyramids. They are overwhelmed by their sheer size and beauty. They are beautiful because they are proportionally harmonious and appealing to our inner as well as our outer feelings.

Gustave Flaubert, in *Letters from Egypt*, 1840, sums it up:

> **"There is something curious about them, these famous pyramids, the more one looks at them, the bigger they become."**

The slopes of the pyramids were not arbitrarily determined for their aesthetic appearance, but as a result of particular geometrical criteria that determined the ratios between their parts – height, edges, base, and so on.

Δ   Δ   Δ

We will take first the Khufu Pyramid.

We begin our investigation with the common understanding of the relationship between form and function.

There are certain undeniable facts about pyramid power. The facts are that if you place highly perishable materials in the so-called "King's Room" of the Khufu (Cheops) Pyramid, or in a similar model of the pyramid, the materials decompose at a much slower rate than if placed anywhere else in the world. Also, people who experiment with blunt, old-fashioned carbon steel razor blades, placing them overnight in a model pyramid, find that the dull blades regain their edges by the next morning.

The evidence from all these experiments is clear: the pyramid shape itself is responsible, somehow, for altering or affecting physical, chemical, and biological processes that take place within a well-proportioned pyramid shape.

The relationship between process and structure—or function and form – applies to a pyramid with harmonic design configuration.

Now we examine harmonic proportion of the Khufu Pyramid, whose design incorporates both:

– The Neb (Golden) Proportion (so-called phi)
– The Circle Index (so-called pi)

This was achieved by a slight variation of several inches in the pyramid's perimeter base.

Some think that it was just a shear coincidence to have the pyramid so harmonically proportioned. But the records of Herodotus, from 2,500 years ago, tell us that the Egyptian priests told him that this pyramid was intentionally designed so that *the area of each face was equal to the square of its height.*

Herodotus' reports are further corroborated by the actual dimensions in Ancient Egyptian units of cubits: 280 for the original height and 440 for the side of the base. The ratio of these two figures [280/220 = h/b = 14/11] <u>corresponds to the square root of the Neb (Golden) Proportion</u>. There is a surprising bonus. Divide twice the base by its height and you get 3.14, a practically perfect value of the Circle Index [commonly known as Pi].

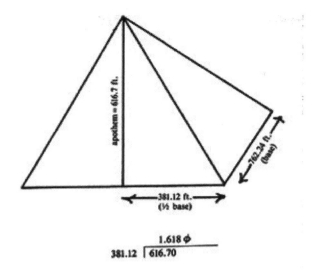

$$381.12 \overline{)\frac{1.618\,\phi}{616.70}}$$

Incorporating the Circle Index into the Pyramid's design is also significant. The angle of elevation of 51° 50' 35" expresses the Circle Index (22/7) with very considerable precision. The angle of ascent gives the pyramid a unique geometrical property that <u>represents the mystic squaring of the circle: that the ratio of the pyramid's perimeter to its height is equal to double the Circle Index.</u>

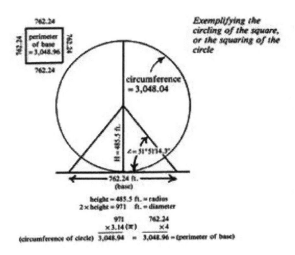

Exemplifying the circling of the square, or the squaring of the circle

Incorporating both these sacred ratios into the design of Egyptian buildings was no coincidence. All Egyptian temples gateways were designed to incorporate both phi and pi—thousands of years before the Greeks.

The typical Ancient Egyptian doorway layout incorporated both sacred ratios (pi and phi), as shown and explained herein.

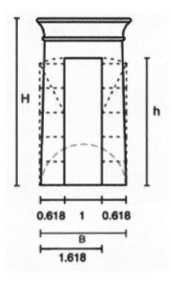

1. The overall outline in the vertical plane is the double-square, 1:2 ratio. [H = 2B]

2. The opening width is based on a square inscribed within a semicircle, the typical Ancient Egyptian way of proportioning a root-five rectangle. Thus, the thickness of the doorjamb is 0.618 the width of the opening.

3. The height of the aperture (h) = 3.1415 = pi

Back to the pyramids of Giza.

The pyramid of Khafra is also a harmonically designed structure. The triangular shape of this pyramid is basically 3:4:5 triangles, side by side, where the height would be 4 units to the base of 6.

Plutarch wrote about the 3:4:5 right-angle triangle of Ancient Egypt in *Moralia, Vol. V*:

> *"**The Egyptians hold in high honor the most beautiful of the triangles**, since they liken the nature of the Universe most closely to it, as Plato in the Republic seems to have made use of it in formulating his figure of marriage. **This triangle has its upright of three units, its base of four, and its hypotenuse of five, whose power is equal to that of the other two sides.** The upright, therefore, may be likened to the male, the base to the female, and the hypotenuse to the child of both, and so Osiris may be regarded as the origin, Isis as the recipient, and Horus as perfected result. Three is the first perfect odd number: four is a square whose side is the even number two; but five is in some ways like to its father, and in some ways like to its mother, being made up of three and two. And panta (all) is a derivative of pente (five), and they speak of counting as "numbering by fives". Five makes a square of itself".*

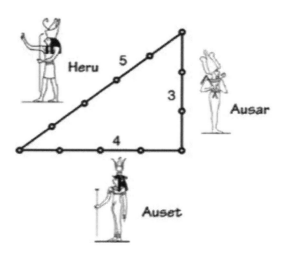

The last pyramid in Giza of Menkaura is, in many ways, *saving the best for last.* Although it is the smallest and youngest of the three pyramids on the Giza Plateau, it has a very interesting harmonic design. Its cross section is very nearly a 5:8 triangle, representing the Neb (Golden) Proportion.

Additionally, the ratio of the height to half the diagonal would be 8:9 (the perfect musical tone), with an angle between the edge and the horizontal of 51° 29' 53". The Menkaura Pyramid ends on a perfect or high note.

>>> So we have seen the intentional harmonic designs of these pyramids and how they relate to the sacred ratios that govern the natural laws dictating the relationship between process and structure.

The Blue house Effect of The Pyramid

The pyramid acts in a similar fashion to the greenhouse effect. The greenhouse effect is basically the retention of heat from sunlight at the earth's surface, caused by atmospheric carbon dioxide that admits shortwave radiation but absorbs the long-wave radiation emitted by the Earth.

The pyramids were harmonically proportioned to act/ function in the same fashion as greenhouses; i.e. to attract and retain certain energies. The shape of a well-proportioned pyramid can concentrate what is called *orgone* energy.

Orgone comes from outer space. It is what makes the stars twinkle, and the sky blue.

Orgone can be accumulated by building a box with wood

on the outside and sheet iron on the inside. The organic material lets the orgone through, and the metal interior reflects it.

This condition/phenomenon could therefore be called the *bluehouse* effect. Abnormally high concentrations of psi-org energy build up inside such a box.

Psi-org combines abbreviations for psychic and orgone energy. They are different names for the same force. The psi field, which produces the human aura and is responsible for all psychic powers, is none other than what Wilhelm Reich, Freud's controversial Austrian disciple, called 'orgone energy'.

The Egyptians knew all about psi-org energy, because they used it. The Ancient Egyptians were the first to discover that the shape of a well-proportioned pyramid can concentrate the psi-org energy.

The bluehouse effect increases drastically when the surface of the pyramid is laminated.

Early historians and travelers told us how the casing stones of the pyramids used to shine. Casing stones were quarried during and after the 13th century, to build mosques and palaces or for burning lime.

The testing of this type of energy was done by Dr. Harald Puton, a very competent Belgian physicist who found that every form of psi energy is increased by sitting under such a harmonically-proportioned pyramid. Such a person is more telepathic, more clairvoyant, and more precognitive. It is easier to initiate out-of-body experiences under these conditions. Additionally, the body's aura is more intense inside a pyramid.

$$\Delta \qquad \Delta \qquad \Delta$$

The Energy channels of Pyramids' Interiors

As stated earlier, the genuine solid stone pyramids have narrow passageways and some empty rooms which are totally devoid of any funerary inscriptions and features.

On the other hand, the later ungenuine heaps of rubble have spacious passageways and burial and offering rooms that are covered with funerary texts.

The interiors of these truly-shaped solid pyramids are basically a network of energy channeling. Such an energy network consists of empty rooms, narrow corridors, large corridors, steep slopes, empty walls, smooth surfaces, etc.

The general characteristics of the true-shaped pyramids during the 4th Dynasty are:

1. From the Meidum Pyramid onward, the entrance to all masonry pyramids was well above ground. The interior rooms were mostly located at the base of the pyramid itself.

2. This and all subsequent masonry pyramids share the same pattern of noticeably low and narrow passages, which lack adequate space to move around or stand up straight.

3. The narrow entrance passage is at a slope of 1:2,

which makes the passage at the diagonal of the sacred double square. The 1:2 rectangle is the most conspicuous element of Egyptian architectural design.

[For more information see the book *The Ancient Egyptian Metaphysical Architecture* by Moustafa Gadalla.]

Δ   Δ   Δ

Energy Centers Versus Abandoned Rooms

Western-minded academicians who made up their minds that the pyramids are tombs and nothing but tombs "explain" all the empty rooms in these magnificent structures as "change of plan and abandonment by the Egyptians"

The abandonment theory is the common escape route for those people, who made up their minds before considering all the evidence. Once they adopted the idea that the pyramids were tombs, they had to twist the evidence to fit into their stubborn theories. In the process, they had no problem fabricating answers.

In the Giza and Dahshur pyramids, which provide no evidence of any kind of burials at all, almost every pyramid, according to this crazy theory, underwent one or several of these peculiar changes of mind. Even odder is the fact that the Giza and Dahshur pyramids are more superior than the pyramids that followed, in every respect: size, workmanship, and elaboration.

It is peculiar that we hear of this abandonment theory only at the best pyramids.

Δ It is worth mentioning that in none of the later ungenuine pyramids used for burials, have the same abandonists claimed that ANY changes of plan took place.

Δ The precision and perfection of everything you see in the Giza and Dahshur Pyramids shows thorough, well thought-out pre-planning.

Δ Just because we don't know the purpose of everything we see, does not give us license to fabricate answers and corrupt history.

Later, when we investigate the interiors of these pyramids, we will discuss the so-called abandoned rooms and changed plans. The evidence is contrary to academia's wild and unfounded notions.

Δ   Δ   Δ

Several photographs in support of the text of this chapter are to be found in the digital edition of this book as published in PDF and E-book formats.

PART IV.

PYRAMID CONSTRUCTION TECHNIQUES

CHAPTER 7.

THE FLAWED "COMMON THEORY"

7.1 THE COMMON 'THEORY'

Many academic Egyptologists claim that there are no Ancient Egyptian records from any period which describes how the pyramids were built. Their error is that they have pre-determined the construction method, and are only seeking the records to affirm their pre-conceived theory. Therefore, they invented a theory. Their 'invented' theory is that:

a. The pyramid's blocks consists of two types:

i. The core blocks which were built mostly of quarried local limestone blocks and cemented by a paper-thin layer of mortar.

ii. An outer casing stones made of fine-grained limestone, which were quarried from Tura on the east bank of the Nile and ferried across the Nile to the site.

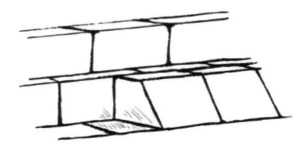

b. To cut and shape the stone blocks, the Egyptians used the following,

　　i. copper chisels and possibly iron tools

　　ii. flint, quartz and diorite pounders

　　iii. large wooden crow bars

c. To transport the stone blocks, they used wooden sledges and rollers. Then the "quarried" stones were hauled up temporary ramps, which increased in both height and length as they were raised to the successive levels of the pyramid.

a. The Unidentified "Source" of Quarried Blocks

Let us consider the following undisputed facts about the Khufu (Cheops) Pyramid of Giza. [Similar facts to those mentioned here are also applicable to all masonry pyramids.]

　　1. The Great Pyramid contains approximately 2.6 million building blocks, weighing from two to seventy tons apiece.

2. Almost none of the pyramid blocks match the Giza bedrock either chemically or mineralogically.

3. The bedrock of the Giza Palteau is made of strata, while the pyramid blocks contain no strata.

4. Strata and defects make it impossible to cut stone to perfectly uniform dimensions.

5. Geologists and geochemists cannot agree on the origin of the pyramid blocks. This alone shatters the common theory that the core masonry of the pyramid was quarried from local bedrock.

6. Natural stone consists of fossil shells which lie horizontally or flat in the bedrock as a result of forming sedimentary layers of bedrock over millions of years. The blocks of the masonry pyramids of Egypt show jumbled shells, which is indicative of manmade, cast stone. In any concrete, the aggregates are jumbled and, as a result, cast concrete is devoid of sedimentary layers. These pyramids essentially consisted of fossil shell limestone, a heterogeneous material very difficult to cut precisely.

7. The French scientists found that the bulk density of the pyramid blocks is 20% lighter than the local bedrock limestone. Cast blocks are always 20-25% lighter than natural rock, because they are full of air bubbles.

b. Cutting and Shaping Impossibilities

1. Stone or copper tools (which are a soft metal), used by Egyptians at that time, cannot cut large granite or

millions of limestone blocks with paper-thin precision, and never within the times allotted for building these pyramids.

2. Limestone frequently splits during cutting. Faults and strata in bedrock assure that for every block cut to standard, at least one will crack or be improperly sized during quarrying.

> >> **Given the many millions of blocks of all these pyramids, there should be millions of cracked blocks lying nearby or somewhere in Egypt; but they are nowhere to be found.**

> In short: no rubbish of cracked blocks means no quarrying. Ancient historians who documented their visits to Egypt have not mentioned heaps of broken blocks.

3. To quarry stones, some suggested that the Egyptians may have heated the surface of the stone to a very high temperature with fire, then sprayed on water to make it split. This suggestion is invalid, because:

> **Firstly**, this method results in providing irregular surfaces and not in making regular-shaped blocks. This method can only be used to reduce large pieces of sandstone, granite, or basalt into small, irregular, fragmented aggregates.

> **Secondly**, heating with fire transfers limestone into lime at 704° (1,300° F). In other words, we no longer have solid pieces of rock. As such, pro-

ducing pyramid blocks by heating limestone is impossible.

4. There are about ten standard block lengths throughout the pyramid. Similarly, limited numbers of standard sizes apply in other pyramids as well. Carving such highly uniform dimensions is impossible. However, having standardized concrete forming molds is a more logical conclusion.

5. Another affirming fact is how long some blocks are. It has been noted that the longest blocks in the pyramids always have the same length. This is extremely strong evidence in favor of the use of casting molds.

c. The Logistics of The Fabricated Ramps' Theory

Δ This is a total invention, but it has been repeated so many times that it became a *fact*, in most peoples' minds.

Δ Herodotus never mentioned such ramps. His historical account described the typical stone causeway between the base of the pyramid and the Valley Temple. This causeway was a permanent feature which was, as Herodotus described, 3300' (1006 m) long, 60' (18 m) wide and 48' (15 m) high, and not used to haul blocks.

Δ Many academicians want to believe that the only way to build the pyramid is by increasing both the height and length of a temporary ramp as it was raised to the successive levels of the pyramid.

Δ The people who are stuck on the ramps theory make reference to what appears to be a mud ramp, found at Sekhemket's Complex in Saqqara. Even if it was a ramp, it was only 23' (7 m) high. The constructed pyramids are much higher than that.

Δ The Danish civil engineer P. Garde-Hanson calculated that to build a ramp all the way to the top of the Khufu Pyramid would require 17.5 million cubic yards (13.4 million cubic meters) of material (7 times the amount needed for the pyramid itself). A workforce of 240,000 would have been needed to build such a ramp, within Khufu's reign of 23 years.

Δ To dismantle the ramp at the completion of Khufu's pyramid would have required a work force of 300,000 and a further eight years. Such a huge amount of rubbish is not visible anywhere in the vicinity and was never mentioned by earlier historians.

Δ After reaching such unbelievable figures, Garde-Hanson theorized a combination of a ramp and a lifting device. He theorized a ramp that would reach halfway up the pyramid. At such a level, about 90 percent of the material needed for the pyramid would have been used. The second element of his modified theory, i.e. the mysterious lifting device of some kind, was and still is an unresolved question.

Hypothetically, let's we agree with Garde-Hanson's theories and try to visualize the staggering figures: 4,000 year-round quarrymen producing 330 blocks per day. During inundation season, 4,000 blocks per day are transported to the Nile, ferried across, hauled up the ramp to the Giza plateau, and set into place in the core—at a rate of 6.67 blocks per minute! Imagine 6.67 blocks every 60 seconds!

This rate is impossible to achieve. This is another reason to disregard the validity of the quarrying and ramp theories.

Δ Building and removing such ramps would have been a much greater task than building any of the pyramids themselves. Therefore, as academicians dream up "primitive means" for Ancient Egyptians, they complicate their own unfounded theories.

Δ   Δ   Δ

7.2 THE FORGOTTEN THREE PYRAMIDS OF SNEFRU

Snefru, during his reign of 24 years, was able to build the two main pyramids at Dahshur as well as a third pyramid at Meidum. This means that he, in the course of his reign of 24 years, was responsible for the production of some nine million tons of stone—several times the quantity of the Great Pyramid of Giza. Even trying to calculate the logistics of such work using modern terms is overwhelming.

Δ   Δ   Δ

7.3 SUMMATION QUESTIONS REFUTING THE WESTERN-MADE "COMMON THEORY"

By not having an open mind, these academicians made it difficult to come up with answers to many questions.

Based on the elements of the "common theory" of stone

cutting, hauling, and hoisting, how can we logically answer the following questions:

1. Where did they get the huge quantity of materials required to build this and other pyramids? There is no physical evidence of such a source, whatsoever?

2. How did they manage to make the sloping sides of the pyramids absolutely flat?

3. How did they make the four sloping sides meet at a perfect point at the summit?

4. How did they make the tiers so level?

5. How did they cut the stones so that they fit together so precisely?

6. What tools did they use?

7. How could the required number of workers (estimated at 240-300,000 people) maneuver on the confined building site?

8. How did they cut the blocks so uniformly?

9. How did they place some of the heaviest blocks in the pyramid, at such great heights?

10. How were 115,000 casing blocks all made to fit to a hair's breadth and closer, as was the case in Khufu's pyramid?

11. How was all the work done in about 20 years?

All these questions invalidate the "common theory".

Common sense, along with physical evidence, lead to the conclusion that the blocks were manmade, as will be explained later on.

>>> Several photographs in support of the text of this chapter are to be found in the digital edition of this book as published in PDF and E-book formats.

CHAPTER 8.

THE MATERIAL FACTS

8.1 HERODOTUS AND PYRAMID CONSTRUCTION

Herodotus neither mentioned the source of the core masonry as local limestone nor that the pyramid blocks were carved. He stated that stones (not necessarily *quarried blocks*, but possibly **stone rubble)** were brought to the site from the east side of the Nile.

Here is an excerpt from Herodotus' account:

> *"This pyramid was built thus; in the form of steps, which some call crosae, and others call bomides. After preparing the foundation, they raised stones by using machines made of short planks of wood, which raised the stones from the ground to the first range of steps. On this range there was another machine which received the stone upon arrival. Another machine advanced the stone on the second step. Either there were as many machines as steps, or there was really only one, and portable, to reach each range in succession whenever they wished to raise the stone higher.*

I am telling both possibilities because both were mentioned."

The term *mechane*, used by Herodotus, is a nonspecific, generic term indicating a type of *device*. When the word *mechane* is translated to mean a device such as a (short blank wooden) mold, the whole description makes sense.

Let us review it in such a form:

"... They raised stones by using molds made of short planks of wood, which raised the stones from the ground to the first range of steps. On this range there was another mold which received the stone [rubble] upon arrival. Another mold advanced the stone on the second step. Either there were as many molds as steps, or there was really only one, and portable, to reach each range in succession whenever they wished to raise the stone higher. I am telling both possibilities because both were mentioned.

A *mold* can be considered as an apparatus or device. If Herodotus was not familiar with the term *'mold'*, he therefore used the more general term, *'mechane'*.

These wooden plank molds have been used in Egypt in various degrees as a molding apparatus to hold the man-made concrete in block-shaped form until the concrete dried.

Δ   Δ   Δ

8.2 EGYPTIAN MOLDING TECHNIQUES

Let us review how the ancient and even some modern

Egyptians make bricks. They push wet Nile mud, mixed with straw and sand, into a wooden mold. Then the soft bricks are set out to dry in the hot sun.

Therefore, using wooden molds to shape the limestone concrete materials into large blocks was nothing new to them.

The Egyptians were very talented carpenters and could manufacture wooden forms with ease.

In Saqqara, we find molded stone blocks in the Step "Pyramid".The very elegant enclosure wall and other buildings, show that molded stones were used to accommodate very elegant and refined architectural details.

Pliny the Elder (23–79 CE), the Roman naturalist, stated in *The Encyclopedia of Natural History, Book 31*, that ***Egyptians made real rocks from a multitude of minerals.***

So, making stones to build a pyramid should not have been a major achievement for them. They had been manufacturing many other stones for a long time. Making stone blocks for pyramids was just another application of their knowledge at that time.

Δ   Δ   Δ

8.3 KHNUM: THE DIVINE MOLDER

There are references to making stones on a stele, commonly known as the "Famine Stele," located on the island of Sehel, near Elephantine, south of Aswan. The stele is dated to about 200 BCE. It is a copy of an Old Kingdom text, which dates to the reign of Zoser, 2,500 years earlier.

The three main characters on the stele are Khnum (who represents the Divine Principle of Molding), King Zoser, and Imhotep.

This stele should have been named *Khnum's Alchemical Stele*, for it holds the key to the method of manufacturing man-made stone.

Approximately one-third of this stele's content pertains to rocks and mineral ore, and their processing. For example, columns 18 and 19 of this Stele quote the Divine Molder, Khnum, speaking to King Zoser:

> ***I am Khnum, your creator ... I give you rare ore after rare ore ... Never before has anyone processed them (to make stone) in order to build the monuments ...***

[For more information about the advanced Ancient Egyptian knowledge of metallurgy and metal alloy fabrication of all types, read *Ancient Egyptian Culture Revealed* by Moustafa Gadalla.]

Δ   Δ   Δ

8.4 SYNTHETIC AND NATURAL BLOCKS

The facts show that these Egyptian pyramid blocks were high-quality, man-made limestone concrete, not quarried natural stone.

The characteristics of the pyramid blocks in Giza are consistent with man-made molded concrete blocks, and can never be of a natural quarry stone.

The case at the Khafra Pyramid gives us the visual evidence.Since the original ground at the Khafra Pyramid was sloping, it was necessary to make it level for the base. As a result, the Egyptians cut the natural ground to provide a level base. You can see the original natural rock of the Giza Plateau. The natural stone has the normal characteristics of formed strata. Strata and defects make it impossible to cut stone to perfectly uniform dimensions. Natural stone consists of fossil shells which lie horizontally or flat in the bedrock, as a result of forming sedimentary layers of bedrock over millions of years.

Next to this exposed bedrock of the Giza Plateau, we can see the formation of the pyramid block that contains no strata whatsoever. The blocks of the masonry pyramids of Egypt show jumbled shells, which are indicative of man-made cast stone. In any concrete, the aggregate are jumbled; and as a result, cast concrete is devoid of sedimentary layers.

Drawing from *Description de l'Egypte*, written between 1809 and 1813 by Francois Jomard, shows jumbled shells in pyramid core blocks.

These pyramids consisted essentially of fossil shell limestone, a heterogeneous material very difficult to cut precisely.

A closer look at the pyramid blocks—like this one—shows us that the top layers of several blocks are quite riddled with holes. The deteriorated layers look like sponges. The denser bottom layer didn't deteriorate. In a concrete mix, air bubbles and excess watery binder rise to the top, producing a lighter, weaker form. The rough top layer is always about the same size, regardless of the height of the block.

This phenomena is evident at all the pyramids and temples of Giza; i.e. light weight, weathered and weak top portions, which is indicative of cast concrete, and not natural stone.

Δ   Δ   Δ

The synthetic blocks consist basically of about 90-95% limestone rubble and 5-10% cement.

It is a known fact that the Ancient Egyptian silico-aluminate cement mortar is far superior to present day hydrated calcium sulfate mortar. By mixing the ancient high quality cement with fossil-shell limestone, the Egyptians were able to produce high quality limestone concrete.

All the required ingredients to make synthetic concrete stone, with no appreciable shrinkage, are plentiful in Egypt:

1. The alumina, used for low temperature mineral synthesis, is contained in the mud from the Nile River.

2. Natron salt (sodium carbonate) is very plentiful in the Egyptian deserts and salt lakes.

3. Lime, which is the most basic ingredient for cement production, was easily obtained by calcining limestone in simple hearths.

4. The Sinai mines contained arsenic minerals, needed to produce rapid hydraulic setting, for large concrete blocks. Natron (a type of flux) reacts with lime and water to produce caustic soda (sodium hydroxide), which is the main ingredient for alchemically making stone.

Records about the source of the arsenic minerals that were used to manufacture the stone are found in Sinai, such as at Wadi Maghara.

Records of mining activities during Zoser's reign are indicated on a stele at the mines of Wadi Maghara in Sinai. Similar mining activities, during the subsequent

Pharaohs' reigns of the 3rd and 4th Dynasties, are also recorded at Sinai.

[For more information about the extensive mining activities in Ancient Egypt as well as advanced Ancient Egyptian knowledge of metallurgy and metal alloy fabrication of all types, read *Ancient Egyptian Culture Revealed* by Moustafa Gadalla.]

Δ   Δ   Δ

8.5 SYNTHETIC CONCRETE BLOCKS VARIOUS TYPES

A man-made concrete is defined as building material made of sand and gravel, bonded together with cement into a hard, compact substance and used in making bridges, road surfaces, etc.

There are countless concrete mixes with varied ratios of the main ingredients: aggregate, cement, water and admixtures. Various applications require different concrete mixes. The Ancient Egyptians utilized a wide variety of concrete mix applications. Examples:

In the Giza Plateau, we can find three types of concrete.

At the Khufu Pyramid, for example, there are three types in the interior pyramid blocks and the exterior angled blocks, as well as the paving blocks around the pyramid site.

The interior pyramid blocks were not intended to be exposed to natural elements. Therefore, they were not finely graded. In other words, they were the bulk-type variety. When the exterior blocks were stripped away, these interior blocks were exposed to the natural elements. Over the years, they have deteriorated rapidly.

The exterior blocks were intended to withstand the natural elements and therefore were made of more finely graded stones, as we can see here from this photograph at the Khafra Pyramid in Giza.

Mastabas throughout the Giza Plateau utilized this strong exterior-type concrete mix in their walls, as shown here in this mastaba-type tomb next to the Great Pyramid.

The third type of concrete mix that we can find at the Giza site is in the paving blocks that surround the base of the pyramid.The exposed paving blocks at the Great Pyramid site show us a finely graded concrete of a quality that can withstand abrasion forces caused by traffic.

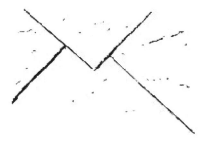

At the Khafra Pyramid site, the paving blocks are in much better shape. They have maintained their superior qualities for thousands of years.

Another application of concrete mixes is the type used by the Egyptians to build their arches and vaulted ceilings. Vaulted ceilings are found, since the Old Kingdom, in Menkaura Pyramid (in Giza) and Mastabat Faroon (in Saqqara). Construction details and quality are found in the Abydos Temple.

Egyptian roofing included various curvatures, just as one can find in the Hatshepsut Temple—Anubis Shrine.

A fourth type of concrete block was used as a harbor water break in Alexandria's outer harbor wall. It predates Alexander, as stated in Greek and Roman classical writings. These were designed to withstand the continuous water pressure forces of waves as well as the effects of salt in the water.

One of the seven wonders of antiquity, the Pharos (lighthouse), at 140 meters high, stood on the island with the same name, in front of the harbor, and showed the way to the ships that carried valuable goods from all over the world.

Δ   Δ   Δ

8.6 THE CASING STONES

Δ The core masonry of the pyramids were dressed with casing blocks made of fine-grained limestone that appears to be polished, and which would have shone brilliantly in the Egyptian sun.

Δ The four sloping faces of the Khufu Pyramid were originally dressed with 115,000 of these casing stones—5.5 acres of them on each of its four faces. Each weighed ten to fifteen tons apiece. The Greek historian Herodotus stated that the joints between them were so finely dressed as to be nearly invisible. A tolerance of .01 inch was the maximum found between these stones—so tight that a piece of paper cannot fit between them.

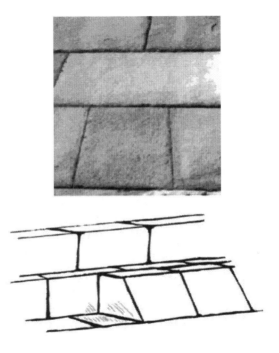

The casing blocks in the 4th Dynasty pyramids were angled to produce the slope of the pyramid. Because of their shape, the casing blocks were cast in an inverted position against neighboring blocks. Once they hardened, the concrete forms were removed and the blocks were then turned upside down and positioned.

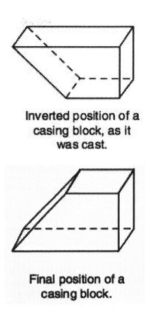

Inverted position of a
casing block, as it
was cast.

Final position of a
casing block.

To reinforce the evidence of such a technique, researchers found that the inscriptions on the casing stones of the Red Pyramid of Snefru and the Khufu (Cheops) Pyramid are always on the bottom of the casing blocks. This is good evidence that they were cast in the inverted position. Had the casing blocks been carved, inscriptions would be found on various sides, and not just one position.

Δ   Δ   Δ

8.7 ADDITIONAL EVIDENTIAL FACTS OF SYNTHETIC PYRAMID BLOCKS

Some earlier points are worth repeating here to complete the context of the subject matter. As stated earlier:

a. There are about ten standard block lengths throughout the pyramid. Similarly, limited numbers of standard sizes apply in other pyramids as well. Carving such highly uniform dimensions is impossible. However, having standardized concrete forming molds is a more logical conclusion.

b. Another affirming fact of how long some blocks are is that the longest blocks in the pyramids always have the same length. This is extremely strong evidence in favor of the use of casting molds.

To add to the evidence that the blocks were are not natural stone but high-quality limestone concrete (synthetic stone) which was cast directly in place, let us consider the following undisputed facts about the Khufu (Cheops) Pyramid of Giza. [Similar facts to those mentioned here are also applicable to all masonry pyramids.]

1. The perfectly fitted millions of blocks can be achieved by molding and forming concrete blocks.

2. In 1974, a team from Stanford Research Institute (SRI) of Stanford University, used electromagnetic sounding equipment to locate hidden rooms. The waves, when sent out, were absorbed by the high moisture content of the blocks. As a result, the mission failed.

> The question is then: How can the pyramid attract moisture in the midst of an arid desert area? The answer is that only concrete blocks retain moisture, which is further evidence showing that the pyramid blocks were synthetic and not quarried.

3. The French scientists found that the bulk density

of the pyramid blocks is 20% lighter than the local bedrock limestone. Cast blocks are always 20-25% lighter than natural rock, because they are full of air bubbles.

4. The paper-thin mortar between the stone blocks does not provide any cohesive power between the stone blocks. This paper-thin mortar is actually the result of excess water in the concrete slurry. The weight of aggregates in the concrete mix squeezes watery cement to the surface, where it sets, to form the thin surface mortar layer.

5. Organic fibers, air bubbles, and an artificial red coating are visible on some blocks. All are indicative of the casting process of man-mad (not natural) stone.

6. The top layers of several blocks are quite riddled with holes. The deteriorated layers look like sponges. The denser bottom layer didn't deteriorate. In a concrete mix, air bubbles and excess watery binder rise to the top, producing a lighter, weaker form. The rough top layer is always about the same size, regardless of the height of the block.

This phenomena is evident at all the pyramids and temples of Giza; i.e. lightweight, weathered, and weak top portions which are indicative of cast concrete, and not natural stone.

7. The largest blocks, found throughout the ancient Egyptian monuments of Giza, exhibit many wavy lines and not horizontal lines. Wavy lines occur when

concrete casting is stopped for several hours (such as an overnight stoppage).

The earlier casted concrete consolidates, and the result is a wavy line that develops between it and the next concrete pour/cast. Strata in the bedrock are horizontal and straight, while wavy lines result when material is poured into a mold.

8. Modern mortar consists exclusively of hydrated calcium sulfate. Ancient Egyptian mortar is based on a silico-aluminate, a result of geopolymerization.

9. These perfectly fitted man-made concrete blocks are not limited to the pyramids, but are found in hundreds of tomb chapels in Giza and elsewhere.

And here we also find no vertical joints and the blocks fit perfectly.

10. The huge paving blocks that surround the pyramids are likewise fitted perfectly—which is made more difficult by the Egyptians' intention of not having continuous cracks. So we have perfectly fitted, huge, irregularly-shaped blocks that can only be made of man-made concrete mix.

11. The only surviving record of the activities of Khnum-Khufu's reign are scenes engraved in Sinai, indicating extensive mining expeditions of arsenic minerals required for making stones.

Δ   Δ   Δ

8.8 THE EARLIER INCREDIBLE MASONRY WORKS OF SAQQARA

A century before the building of the 4th Dynasty great pyramids, an even more impressive greater stonework monument was built in Saqqara. It was the Complex of Zoser. The Step "Pyramid" of Zoser is located within the boundaries of the Pyramid Complex of Zoser. This complex was built during the reign of King Zoser (2630-2611 BCE).

The Complex contains, in addition to the Step "Pyramid", several buildings, colonnades and temples. The whole Zoser Complex is a masterpiece of harmony and order.

The Complex is a perfect double square, whose walls are oriented exactly along the cardinal directions.

The Saqqara Zoser Complex contains at least one million tons of stone.

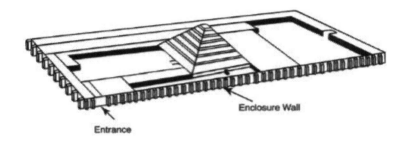

The Pyramid Complex of Zoser

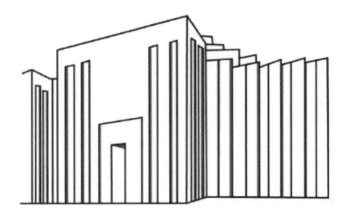

The Enclosure Wall of Zoser's Complex

The amount of stone used in the Zoser Complex (such as the enclosure wall) indicates a mastery of stone making before the time of Khufu (Cheops). Therefore, this Complex deserves more attention than the Great Pyramids of Giza.

The enclosure wall is a part of the Zoser Complex that King Zoser built. It surrounds an area of more than a square mile. When complete, the enclosure wall was 1,000 cubits (nearly 600 yards, 549 m) long, and 500 cubits (300 yards, 274 m) wide, and rose to a height of over 30' (9.1 m). It is built of limestone and faced with finely polished limestone.

The enclosure wall's successive recesses and projections required more than triple the amount of both stone and labor of a similarly-sized simple (flat) wall.

This enclosure wall has 14 bastion gates, but only one is real. The other 13 are simulated. The Complex is a perfect double square, whose walls are oriented exactly along the cardinal directions.

[More about the complex, unique architecture, functions, etc. in *The Ancient Egyptian Metaphysical Architectire* by Moustafa Gadalla.]

Δ   Δ   Δ

There are several other monuments near the Zoser Complex in Saqqara, such as the Pyramid Complex of Sekhemket (2611–2603 BCE), west of the Unas Structure, where we find stone blocks spread over a wide area. The stone blocks here are similar in size to Zoser's Superstructure ("pyramid"). To confirm that the blocks were man-made, they found the Pharaoh's name (Sekhemket) on monuments in Sinai, near the mine sites of the arsenic minerals which are needed to make limestone blocks.

Δ   Δ   Δ

>>> Several photographs in support of the text of this chapter are to be found in the digital edition of this book as published in PDF and E-book formats.

PART V.

THE THREE SNEFRU PYRAMIDS

CHAPTER 9.

SNEFRU'S MEIDUM PYRAMID

9.1 THE EXTERIOR

Snefru's Meidum Pyramid is the most southern masonry pyramid.

As one gets closer to Meidum, one sees the outline of a strange structure which does not look like a pyramid at all. It looks more like kind of a high, stepped tower, rising out of a tremendous heap of rubble.

This is the remains of the collapsed Pyramid of Meidum:

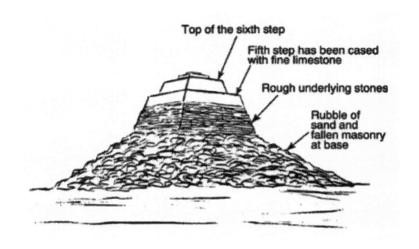

Top of the sixth step

Fifth step has been cased with fine limestone

Rough underlying stones

Rubble of sand and fallen masonry at base

Δ As is always the case with true-shaped Egyptian pyramids, this one is also devoid of any inscriptions or references. Several graffiti on and around the ruins indicate that the Egyptians themselves ascribed it to King Snefru (2575–2551 BCE). Despite this fact, some people guessed that the pyramid was built, or mostly built, by Huni (2599–2575 BCE), the last of the 3rd Dynasty Kings. King Huni's name is not mentioned anywhere in the area.

All circumstantial evidence indicates that Snefru alone built it. But the people who insist that the pyramids were tombs and nothing else could not deal with Snefru having three pyramids which, in their minds, means three tombs.

This is the reason they came up with the unfounded story that Huni built (or mostly built) this pyramid.

Δ The Meidum Pyramid of Snefru:

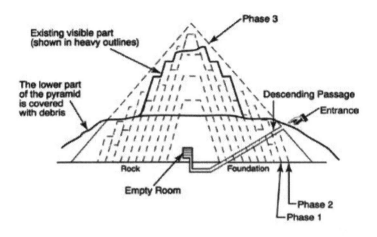

Height (original): 306' (93m)
Mass (original?): 1.5 million tons
Base (original): 482' (147m) square
Angle: 51° 50' 35"

Δ After the pyramid was completed, a few of the casing blocks were squeezed out of place, a chain reaction followed, and the entire outer casing gave way. Much of the core masonry was pulled with the loose casing stones. As a result of this avalanche, a huge rubble heap was formed around the pyramid. This explains its tower-like appearance.

>> The presence of the Pyramid Temple (wrongly known as a mortuary temple) next to the collapsed pyramid proves that the collapse occurred after the pyramid was completed. They would not have built this temple next to the pyramid if the pyramid actually collapsed during con-

struction. To build a temple next to a collapsed pyramid would have been a moot and dangerous undertaking.

Δ The blocks of this pyramid weigh about 550 pounds (250 kg). There is no evidence of these stone blocks being quarried locally or otherwise. On the other hand, records in the mines of Sinai indicate vigorous activities during Snefru's reign. Such records show that arsenic minerals, needed for the production of man-made limestone blocks, were extracted.

Δ This collapsed pyramid that looks like a tower is a reminder of the *Tower of Babel*. The biblical tale of the fall of the *Tower of Babel* was probably a garbled folk memory of the collapse of the Meidum Pyramid. It was also believed that the original seven steps of the pyramid conformed to the seven planets and their associated seven musical sounds. The additional eighth step was contrary to sacred scripts and may have been the reason it collapsed.

> **This first known true pyramid has the same harmonic proportions (but with different dimensions) as the later-built Great Pyramid of Giza of Khufu's; it has the same angle between the face and the base of the pyramid.**

Detailed explanations will be shown in a later chapter dealing with the Great Pyramid of Giza.

9.2 THE INTERIOR

Here in the pyramid at Meidum, the passages are very confining for human use:

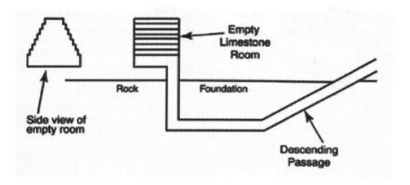

Notice the unique arrangement of the passages in this pyramid. Access to the only small room in the pyramid can only be achieved via a narrow vertical shaft, as shown in above diagram.

The only entrance to the pyramid is high above ground level.

Then we have the steep 2:1 sloped narrow passage-way—which can only be passable by the modern installation of wooden ramps and rails.

The inclined narrow passageway becomes horizontal before a 900 vertical up shaft [which is only 3.8' x 2.8' (117 x 85 cm) wide] leads to a very small, empty room.

>> **This small, empty room had no inscriptions. The room is [and always was] totally empty. There was never a sarcophagus or a stone chest there, because it would have had to be placed in the room at the time when it was being built, and it could not have left the room by the narrow shaft unless it was broken into pieces. No granite fragments of a stone chest were found, either in the room itself or anywhere in the corridor.**

Δ This room has a fine corbelled roof—fashioned like steps in reverse—composed of seven steps.

Exactly similar to the later Khufu's pyramid in Giza.

The collapsed pyramid at Meidum is the first of 3 pyramids built by Snefru, who preceded Khufu.

>>> Various photographs in support of the text of this chapter are to be found in the digital edition of this book as published in PDF and E-book formats.

CHAPTER 10.

SNEFRU'S BENT PYRAMID

The other two pyramids built during Snefru's reign are located in Dahsur, which is about 30 miles (50 km) north of his Collapsed Pyramid of Meidum. The two pyramids of Dahshur are less than a mile (1.6 km) apart.

In this chapter we will study the Bent Pyramid [also called the Northern pyramid of Dahshur], and in the next chapter we will study the Red Pyramid.

10.1 THE EXTERIOR

Δ The Bent Pyramid has a double-angled profile and two totally separate sets of rooms, one entrance on the customary north side, and a second entrance on the west side.

Δ As is the case in all true-shaped pyramids, this pyramid is again totally devoid of any markings.

This pyramid was attributed to King Snefru (2575–2551 BCE), based on a reference to his name in the nearby temple.

Δ The blocks here vary in size. Such variety in sizes provides for better interlocking,which ensures the stability of the structure.

Δ Snefru's Bent Pyramid:
Base: 602' (184 m) square   Height: 344' (105 m)
Mass: 3.6 million tons   Inclination: 53° 27'
base; 43° 22' 44" top

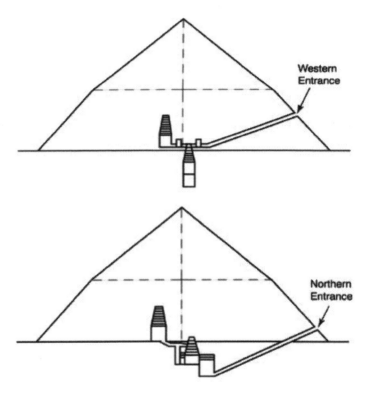

Δ The evidence inside the Bent Pyramid leads us to conclude that its unique double angle was a deliberately planned design, since:

– The early stages of construction reflected that these

separate entrances, corridors, and underground rooms were part of the original plan.

– The emphasis upon a dual purpose or dual symbolism for this pyramid seems more reasonable than attempting to explain it as yet another change of plan.

– The French Egyptologist, Varille, stated that two slopes for each side of this pyramid had been designed this way intentionally, with the aim of obtaining a certain geometrical ratio between the ground-level section and the middle section of the pyramid.

10.2 THE INTERIORS

Δ The system of passages are consistent with true Egyptian pyramids that contain steep and narrow passageways with inaccessible, small, empty rooms.

Shown below are two views of this internal system, showing this very unique and mysterious arrangement of empty, steep, narrow, and small passageways, shafts, and rooms.

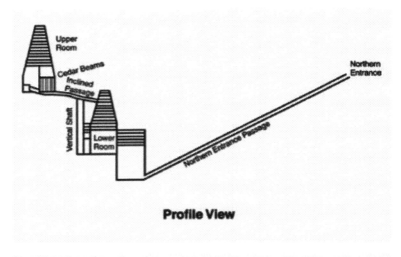

Profile View

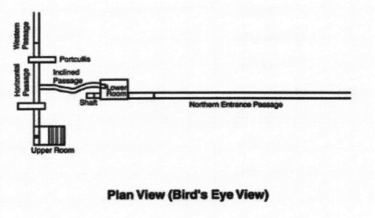

Plan View (Bird's Eye View)

△ The descending passage from the northern entrance is 3'-7" (1.1 m) high. Again, like Meidum, the passage is too small for any person to walk up straight, and it follows the diagonal of a 1:2 rectangle.

△ The passageway leads to two internal rooms, which have corbel roofs. There is no trace of a stone chest or of a burial taking place in either room.

Δ A second passage connects the upper room with an opening high up in the western face of the pyramid. This passageway is also 3'-7" (1.1 m) high, which is too small for standing up.

>>> Various photographs in support of the text of this chapter are to be found in the digital edition of this book as published in PDF and E-book formats.

CHAPTER 11.

SNEFRU'S RED PYRAMID

11.1 THE EXTERIOR

Δ A mile away from the Bent Pyramid, we find the third pyramid that was built by Snefru—the Red Pyramid.

It is popularly called the Red Pyramid because of the reddish or pinkish tint of its core stone.

This is the earliest monument that is in complete pyramidal form. It is still in a good condition because it still retains large areas of its original casing stones.

Δ The blocks here are huge. The height of blocks here vary from 1'-7" (.5 m) to 4'-7" (1.4 m).

Δ The geometric configuration of this pyramid is interesting since the inclination of the face of the pyramid is exactly like the upper section of the Bent Pyramid.

Δ Snefru's Red Pyramid

  Height: 341' (104 m)
  Base: 722' square (220 m)

Mass: 4.0 million tons
Inclination: 43° 22' 44"

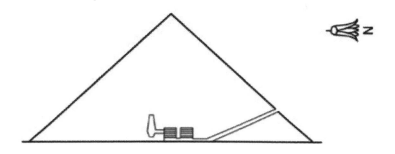

11.2 THE INTERIORS

△ The entrance passage is again the unique typical diagonal of a 1:2 rectangle. It leads down a long, sloping corridor to the bedrock, and is only 3'-11" (1.2 m) high – too small for a person to walk standing up straight.

Leading to a narrow horizontal corridor:

This opens into two adjoining identical rooms with typical corbelled roofs:

A short passage leads upward to a third room. The corbelled roof of this third room rises to a height of 50' (15.2 m).

△ All rooms aretotally empty, and like the rest of all interiors are totally devoid of any inscriptions.

△ No traces of a stone chest or burial were found anywhere in the three rooms.

Δ Also here, for the first time, the rooms were incorporated into the pyramid itself (traditionally, they were located at the base of the pyramid itself).

Δ   Δ   Δ

Δ Δ Δ Snefru built three colossal pyramids and erected stone monuments throughout Egypt. It is estimated that nine million tons of stone were used during the Pharaoh's 24-year reign.

Δ Δ Δ Snefru used more stone in building than the famous Khufu. Building with stone occurred on a much larger scale prior to the building of Khufu's Great Pyramid at Giza. Let us also not forget the big project of the Zoser Complex at Saqqara.

Δ Δ Δ There is no evidence of burial in any of the three pyramids. It should be clearer than ever that these pyramids were not built to entomb anybody.

>>> Various photographs in support of the text of this chapter are to be found in the digital edition of this book as published in PDF and E-book formats.

PART VI.

THE THREE PYRAMIDS
OF GIZA

CHAPTER 12.

THE GIZA PLATEAU

The Giza Plateau is the location of three pyramids built by the three pharaohs who succeeded Snefru and his three pyramids.

The Giza Plateau is an enormous and impressive site. The following are the main features of the Giza Plateau:

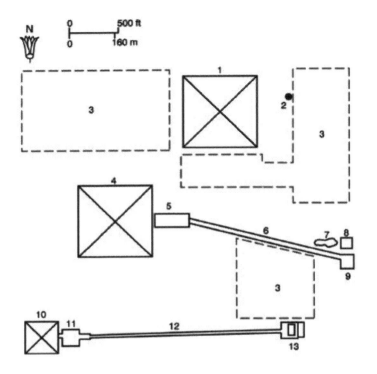

1. Great Pyramid of Khufu (Cheops).
2. Tomb of Queen Hetepheres.
3. Mastaba fields.
4. Pyramid of Khafra (Chephren).
5. Pyramid Temple of Khafra.
6. Causeway to Valley Temple of Khafra.
7. Great Sphinx.
8. Temple of the Sphinx.
9. Valley Temple of Khafra.
10. Pyramid of Menkaura (Mycerinus).
11. Pyramid Temple of Menkaura.
12. Menkaura Causeway.
13. Valley Temple of Menkaura.

Our main focus now will be the three Giza pyramids.

The subject of the Great Sphinx is elaborated on in our publication *Ancient Egyptian Culture Revealed* by Moustafa Gadalla.

CHAPTER 13.

KHUFU'S GREAT PYRAMID

13.1 THE EXTERIOR

The Great Pyramid of Khufu (Cheops) is the largest of all the pyramids.

The main construction features of this pyramid are:

Δ The pyramid consists of 203 steps. The heights of the steps continually decrease from bottom to top. However, there are hundreds of blocks weighing from 15 to 30 tons situated near the "King's" Room. Blocks of this size are so large that they occupy the space of two tiers.

Δ The pyramid was surrounded by and built partly upon a pavement or platform of limestone blocks, portions of which can be seen at the northern and eastern sides.

Δ Its base area is approximately 13 acres (53,000 sq. meters), enough to hold the cathedrals of Florence, Milan and St. Peters as well as Westminster Abbey and St. Paul's.

Height (Original): 280 cubits (481', 147m)

Base: 440 cubits square (757' sq, 229m sq)
Mass: 6.5 million tons of limestone
Area of base: 13 acres (5.3 hectares)
Inclination: 51° 50' 35"

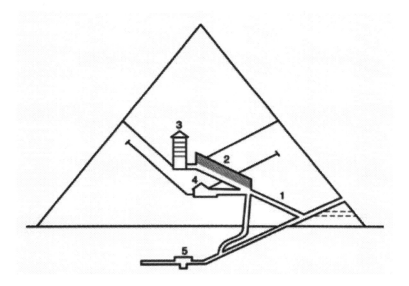

1. **Ascending Passage**
2. **Grand Gallery**
3. **"King's" Room**
4. **"Queen's" Room**
5. **Subterranean Room**

Δ   Δ   Δ

>> It should be noted that its geometric relationship between the four faces and the base are exactly the same as the Collapsed Pyramid of Snefru at Meidum.

>> The pyramid was designed to intentionally incorporate both:

– The Neb (Golden) Proportion (so-called phi)

– The Circle Index (so-called pi)

This was achieved by a slight variation of several inches in the perimeter base of the pyramid.

Δ Some think that it was just a shear coincidence to have the pyramid so harmonically proportioned. But we have the records of Herodotus 2,500 years ago telling us that the Egyptian priests told him that this pyramid was **intentionally designed so that the area of each face was equal to the square of its height.**

Δ Herodotus' reports are further corroborated by the actual dimensions in the Ancient Egyptian units of cubits: 280 for the original height and 440 for the side of the base. The ratio of these two figures [280/220 = h/b = 14/11] corresponds to the square root of the Neb (Golden) Proportion, as follows:

- **Height / ½ Base = 280 /220 = 14/11 = 1.272727**

- **Square of 1.272727 = 1.619 = Golden Ratio**

Δ There is a surprising bonus. Divide twice the base by the height and you get 3.14: a practically perfect value of the Circle Index.

- **2 Base / Height = 880/ 280 = 3.1429 = Circle Index**

- **3.14159 – 3.1429 = 0.0013**

   Difference = 0.04%

Δ Incorporating the Circle Index into the Pyramid's

design is also significant. The angle of elevation of 51° 50′ 35″, expresses the Circle Index (22/7) with very considerable precision. **The angle of ascent gives the pyramid a unique geometrical property that represents the mystical squaring of the circle: that the ratio of the pyramid's perimeter to its height is equal to double the Circle Index.**

[For more information about 'squaring the circle' in Ancient Egypt, refer to the book *The Ancient Egyptian Metaphysical Architecture* by Moustafa Gadalla.]

Δ Δ Δ **This, however, is not the first time that the Ancient Egyptians used these important relationships, because Snefru's Pyramid at Meidum has the same geometric characteristics as Khufu's (Cheops') Pyramid.**

Δ Δ Δ **Incorporating both these sacred ratios into the design of Egyptian buildings was no coincidence. All Egyptian temple gateways were designed to incorporate both phi and pi—thousands of years before the Greeks.**

The typical Ancient Egyptian doorway layout incorporated both sacred ratios (pi and phi), as shown and explained earlier in this book.

Δ   Δ   Δ

13.2 KNUM-KHUFU

The building of this pyramid is attributed to King Khnum-Khufu, who is generally known as Khufu (Cheops), and who reigned from 2551–2528 BCE.

The name Khnum-Khufu is significant because Khnum, as explained earlier, represents the Divine Molder. This is significant because it relates to the method of making stones by molding/casting them.

The Attribution of Khnum-Khufo is based on:

1. The inscriptions in the mastabas surrounding the pyramid make several references to the name of Khnum-Khufu.

2. The Greek historian, Herodotus, attributed this pyramid to Khnum-Khufu, based on the information provided to him by his priest informants.

Δ   Δ   Δ

13.3 THE INTERIOR

Look at the Great Pyramid of Giza built by Khufu.

Let us get familiar with the interiors of this pyramid.

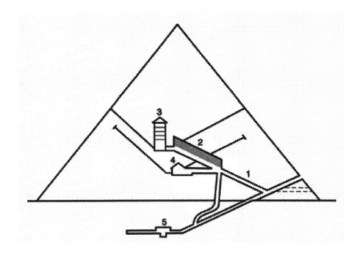

1. Ascending Passage
2. Grand Gallery
3. "King's" Room
4. "Queen's" Room
5. Subterranean Room

13.3.A. ENTERING THE PYRAMID

The entrance to this and all other TRUE pyramids are on the north side.

>> **The true entrance was covered with stone blocks for thousands of years, and therefore was invisible.**

As for historical references, Herodotus did not mention any passages. The Greco/Roman historian, Strabo (1st century CE) reported that *the pyramid entrance was concealed behind a secret stone, indistinguishable from the others.*

Δ The present entrance that is being used by all entrees is so rough-looking. This is actually the entrance of the forced passage.

The original entrance is that aperture beneath the huge limestone gables, located higher up and to the left of the forced entrance.

People had been trying to enter the pyramid for thousands of years, looking for possible gold and treasures.

In the 9th century the Arab Caliph Al Mamun, unaware of the original entrance, forced his way through the solid stone in the sixth course of masonry, which led him to the first interior passage of the pyramid. Only then, by tracking this interior passage, was he able to find the location of the true original entrance. The stone blocks covering the entrance were then removed.

Below is what the forced passage looks like—which leads to the descending passage.

The forced passage which Al Mamun cut was 118′ (36 m) long before he reached the junction of the original descending and ascending passages.

>> **There is no evidence whatsoever, either on the outer surfaces of the pyramid or inside it, which suggests that someone had broken into the pyramid earlier than Al Mamun.**

>> **At the end of the forced entry, we can see how the ascending passageway was totally blocked at the true entryway to the pyramid.**

The true entrance was therefore totally blocked from the inside, as well as the outside, by indistinguishable exterior pyramid blocks.

The Two Entrances [plan and profile]

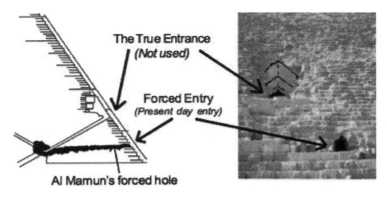

Δ   Δ   Δ

13.3.B. THE DESCENDING PASSAGE AND SUBTERRANEAN ROOM

Δ At the end of Al Mamun's forced passageway, one reaches the pyramid's descending passage, which starts from the original and only intended entrance to the pyramid.

Δ Again, the descending passage has the usual steep and narrow 2:1 slope. It is only 3'-6" (1.1 m) wide and 3'-11" (1.2 m) high.

Δ This descending passage runs exactly north-south (i.e. it is meridional).

Δ The passage is 345' (105 m) long, plus the 29' (8.83 m) horizontal corridor to where the Subterranean Room is located.

Δ **The descending passage** goes down below the base of the pyramid and into the bedrock, to the Subterranean Room.

Khufu pyramid (Partial profile view).

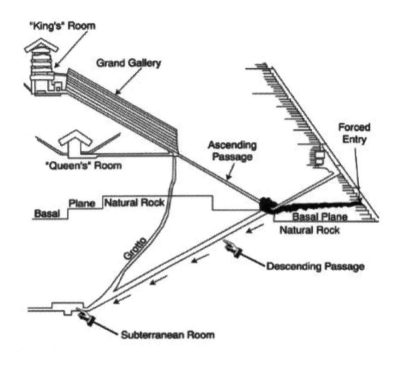

Δ   Δ   Δ

The Subterranean Room is located 600′ (183 m) below the apex of the pyramid. It is a very crude room, void of any inscriptions. It measures about 46′ x 27′-1″ x 11′-6″ (14 x 8.3 x 3.5 m). Nobody knows the purpose of it, but that didn't stop many from making up answers.

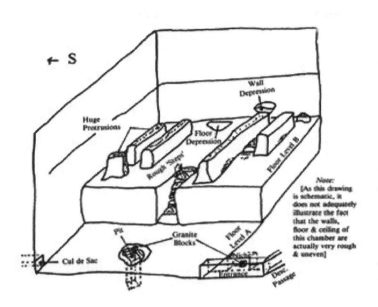

Δ Some theorize that the Subterranean Room was intended to bury the King and that the Egyptians changed the plan, abandoned it, and chose what is now the "Queen's" Room. Then these same people theorized again about another change in plan, in which the Egyptians abandoned the "Queen's" Room for the "King's" Room.

Δ There is no evidence, physical or otherwise, that there was any change in plan, anyplace in this pyramid.

Δ It is possible that this room was simply a part of energy channeling network for this pyramid.

Δ It could be that this room was in existence before the pyramid was even built.

Δ   Δ   Δ

13.3.C. ASCENDING PASSAGE

Proceeding up the confined ascending passage, one encounters a very restricted low ceiling. This passage is only 3'-11" (1.2 m) high and 3'-6" (1.1 m) wide, and rises at a 26 ½° angle (2:1 typical slope).

The ascending passage is only 129' (39 m) long, but it will seem much longer when you are going through this confining passageway.

Δ This ascending passage runs exactly in a north-south direction i.e. it is meridional.

Δ The walls are devoid of any inscriptions and/or drawings, like the previous pyramids.

Δ **The passage is too low and narrow to walk upright.**

Δ The original floor is very slippery. With the inevitable sand on top of the floor, it would be almost impossible to keep from sliding the whole way down.

Δ In the 1940s, handrails and wooden ramps with metal footings were installed. It is also electrically lit inside these days.

Δ   Δ   Δ

13.3.D. "QUEEN'S" ROOM CORRIDOR

Let us re-orient ourselves again:

Δ The ascending passage branches into the Grand
Gallery, and another horizontal branch leads to the so-
called "Queen's Room".

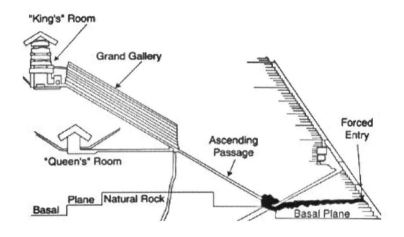

At the juncture of the ascending and horizontal passages

there is a shaft opening, which descends partly vertically and partly at a very steep angle to a depth of 197' (60 m).

It opens into the lower part of the descending passage.

Δ Here we are looking back at the ascending passage. We are ready to go through yet another narrow passage. Let us continue in the horizontal passage, where it ends at the so-called "Queen's Room".

Δ Always notice the total absence of any inscription or depiction in the interiors of all these TRUE pyramids.

The horizontal corridor is so small that one must almost crawl inside it.

Crawling inside the "Queen's" Room corridor

The low and narrow passage is only 3'-11" (1.2 m) high, and 3'-6" (1.1 m) wide. This is hard on the back. It is too small again.

The corridor is 127' (39 m) long, and is located in the central mass of the core masonry.

As we approach the limestone gabled room, there is a

mysterious sudden drop in the floor of 1'-7" (0.5 m) towards the end of the passage.

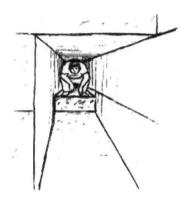

The drop is an intentional design feature whose purpose could be simply that it was a part of the energy channeling scheme for this pyramid.

Those who say that "it was a change in plan" present the academic standard "escape route" when they don't understand something.

Δ   Δ   Δ

13.3.E. THE "QUEEN'S" ROOM

Here is the entrance to the so-called "Queen's Room"—even though all scholars agree that nobody was ever buried here.

Δ The "labeling" of the room as "Queen's Room" was an arbitrary labeling by the Arabs who broke into the pyramid.

Δ The room is made entirely of limestone walls with plaster over them. The floor has been left rough.

Δ This room lies exactly on the pyramid's east-west axis.

Δ This room was always empty, and all the scholars agree that nobody was ever buried here.

Δ As usual throughout the TRUE pyramids, the walls are totally devoid of any inscriptions or depictions.

Δ Some suggested that this room was built to bury the King, and the Egyptians changed their plan for the second time. (The first time was the Subterranean Room below the base of the pyramid.)

There is no basis whatsoever for such wild assumptions. On the contrary, the physical evidence contradicts such a wild notion. We have two small and long channels here, which are incorrectly labeled as *air shafts*.

They are about 8″ x 8″ (20 cm x 20 cm) in cross-section. Both channels are sealed at both ends. These channels were added to the core masonry, level by level as the pyramid went up.

If the Egyptians abandoned this room for what is now called the "King's" Room, there was no reason whatsoever to extend the channels of the "Queen's" Room beyond the floor level of the "King's" Room. But they did.

The southern channel was extended 64′ (19.5 m) higher than the floor level of the "King's" Room; i.e. it ran almost parallel to the southern channel of the "King's" Room for 82′ (25 m) of its track.

Δ The two channels, one directed to the north and the other to the south, do not run through to the outside of the pyramid, proving that they were not intended *to ventilate* the room, as some have supposed.

Δ They were called "ventilation shafts" because nobody knew what else to call them.

Δ The northern channel has many kinks in it because it goes around the Grand Gallery.

There was no mistake then in the alignment of the northern channel, because the same situation occurred again at the "King's" Room, several courses above the "Queen's" Room.

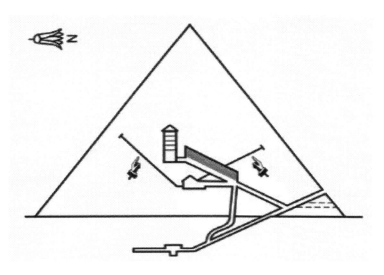

Orientation of the two channels in the "Queen's" Room

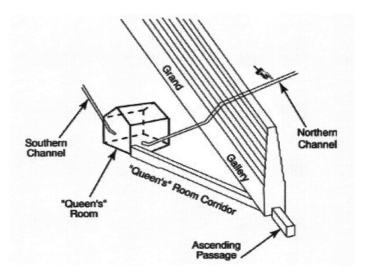

Kink in Northern Channel

Δ   Δ   Δ

13.3.F. THE GRAND GALLERY

The Grand Gallery is reached after going back from the "Queen's" Room through the horizontal corridor, towards the end of the ascending passage.

If you remember, we went through the steep, narrow, ascending passage.

Δ The very confined Ascending passage leads to the Grand Gallery, which is very spacious, even though it is still as steep as the ascending passage. Like all internal passages, the slope of this gallery is the diagonal of a 1:2 rectangle.

Δ A modern wooden ramp has been placed over the polished and smooth floor, making it much easier to climb. Without this, it would be impossible to walk up the smooth, sloped surface.

Δ The gallery is a beautiful masterpiece that is 157' (48 m) long, 29' (85 m) high, and 62" (1.6 m) wide at the bottom, and 41" (1 m) wide at the top, with a corbelled roof design consisting of seven inverted steps—**exactly as we have seen in the earlier pyramids by King Snefru.**

Δ Again, just like all the interiors of this [and all other] true-shaped solid pyramids, the walls are totally devoid of any drawings and/or inscriptions.

Δ   Δ   Δ

Immediately before one reaches the upper end of the Gallery, there is a 3' (1 m) step; then it levels off.

At the top of the southern wall (at the upper end of the Gallery) is a small opening that leads to a forced passage, made to reach the area referred to as Davison's Room, atop the granite roof of the "King's" Room.

At the upper end of the Gallery, this very spacious and gorgeous Grand Gallery ends. At the top of the Grand Gallery, we are faced with a very narrow and short opening, and it is time to crawl on hands and knees, again, towards the "King's" Room.

This short, confined space is followed by a spacious area, and then we are back again in a very narrow passage.

That leads to the granite room—erroneously popularized
as the "King's Room".

Δ   Δ   Δ

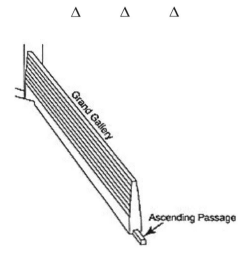

The Grand Gallery

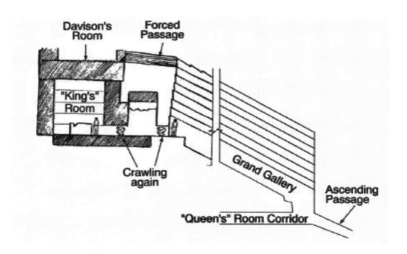

The Grand Gallery, Leading to the "King's" Room

13.3.G. THE "KING'S" ROOM

Δ **The restricted opening space to the Room is smaller than the granite and lidless box which looks like (but is not) a sarcophagus that is located at the other end of the Room. The physical evidence is very clear that this granite and lidless box was placed here prior to completing the construction of this room.**

Δ A profile of this room and its connection to the spacious grand gallery shows us two very restrictive areas that will require almost crawling in between the gallery and the granite (the so-called King's Room).

Δ Herodotus never mentioned the existence of this or any rooms or passageways in the pyramid.

Δ This room is constructed entirely of monoliths of smooth granite.

Δ The walls here are formed of five courses containing exactly one hundred granite blocks.

Δ Each monolith weighs 30 tons and all these blocks are perfectly smooth-faced. No mortar was used to join them.

Δ They are so perfectly fitted that a knife could not pass between them. This is incredible, for such a weight and such a fit.

Δ The ceiling is formed of nine immense monoliths: some of them weighing over 50 tons.

Atop the roof of the "King's" Room

Δ Above the roofing slabs, there are a series of rough-hewn granite blocks which contain five compartments. The space above the "King's" Room was named Davison's Room, after its discoverer Nathanael Davison.

Δ Some thought that this particular roof design was probably made to reduce the pressure from the colossal weight of the stone above.

This theory is not convincing because the lower "Queen's" Room is subject to greater stress; yet it does not have this roof design.

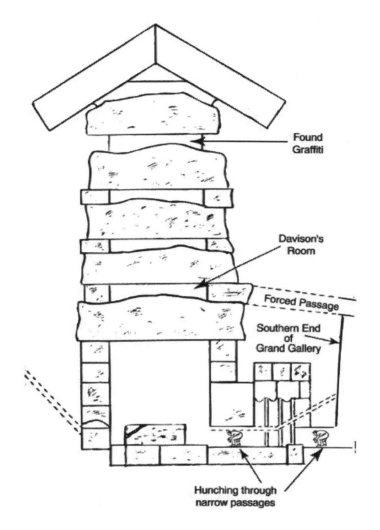

The "King's" Room

Δ   On one of the upper slabs is some graffiti with the
     name of Khufu (Cheops). This is the only reference
     to Khufu inside the pyramid. It is even questionable
     if such graffiti was carved during Khufu's era or by a
     modern-day visitor. The pyramid is totally devoid of
     any official inscriptions.

Δ At the western end of the room is the mysterious empty, lidless chest, made of very smooth granite. No inscription on it whatsoever.

Δ The granite chest has been badly damaged by souvenir hunters who chipped pieces from its edges.

>> **The passageway into the room is too narrow to pass this granite chest. Therefore, it had to have been placed in the room as the pyramid was being built.**

Δ There is not the slightest evidence of a corpse having been in this room; not a sign of funerary material or fragment of any artifact. No clue, however minuscule, has ever been found in this room or anywhere else in the Great Pyramid, to indicate that a *burial* took place here.

Δ The "King's" Room.

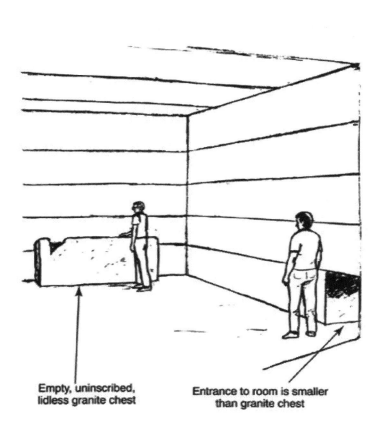

Empty, uninscribed, lidless granite chest

Entrance to room is smaller than granite chest

Δ Notwithstanding all other reasons, if we assume for a moment that this room was used for the dead Pharaoh's mummy, then they must have placed this oversized granite chest in the room during the construction of the pyramid.

Then, when the King died, they must have dragged his dead body up these difficult passages and squeezed it through the narrow constrictions, to place the mummy into the uninscribed granite chest!

>> **If people look at all these physical facts, it becomes**

quite obvious that the tomb theory is insulting to our intelligence.

Δ Not even a portion of a lid for this granite chest was ever found in any of the pyramid passages or rooms.

Hypothetically, if we assume that the robbers made it to this room to steal the contents, they might have smashed the lid; but they would hardly have taken the trouble to steal a broken lid. Despite a careful search, no chips of a broken granite lid have been found anywhere in the pyramid passages or rooms.

Δ **The labeling of this room as "King's Room" is/was [as is the case with the so-called "Queen's Room"] arbitrary—made by the Arabs who broke into the pyramid.** The Arab savages labeled it a "King" room with no basis whatsoever for this designation.

Δ The walls and the granite chest are (and always were) totally devoid of any inscriptions.

Δ   Δ   Δ

Δ This room is simple yet powerful. The most obvious design significance is that its configuration/proportion manifests the knowledge of Ancient Egyptian sacred geometry in three-dimensional architecture.

> 1. The floor plan of the room is a double square (2 x 1 rectangle), 20 x 10 Egyptian cubits (34'-4" x 17'-2", 10.5 x 5.2 m).

> 2. The double square, divided by a single diagonal CA, forms two right triangles; each having a

base of 1 and a height of 2. The diagonal CA is equal to the square root of 5 (2.236) – i.e. 22.36 cubits in actual length.

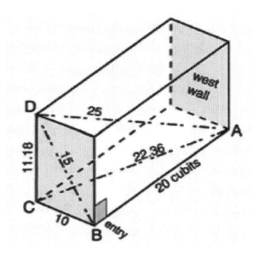

3. The height of the room is designed to be one half the length of the floor diagonal CA, i.e. √5/2, which is 11.18 cubits (19'-2" or 5.8 m) in actual length.

4. This choice of CD, as the height of the room, will make the diagonal DB (in the triangle DCB) equal to 15 cubits. The result is that the three sides of the triangle ABD are in relation to 3:4:5.

5. The harmonic proportion of this room shows the intimate relationship between 1:2:3:4:5, and demonstrates the relationship in the divine harmonic proportion (sacred geometry) between process and structure.

6. It also shows that the right-angle triangle prin-

ciple (so-called Pythagoras) was regularly practiced in Egyptian design, some 2,000 years
before Pythagoras walked this earth.

Δ   Δ   Δ

**Attention is drawn to the holes in the north and south
walls, erroneously known as "air shafts."**

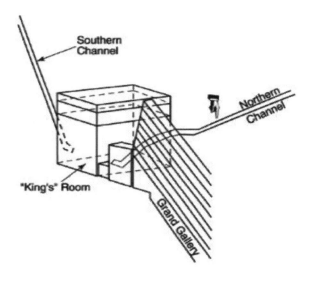

Kink in Northern Channel

There are channels in this room which have the same
configuration as the ones in the "Queen's" Room; i.e.
approximately 8″ x 8″ (20 cm x 20 cm).

Both channels, here, emerge on the exterior of the pyramid; unlike the channels in the "Queen's" Room, which do
not go all the way through the exterior.

Calling these shafts "air shafts" is baseless and against all logic. Both inclined channels start about 3′ (1 m) above floor level, where a vent logically starts at the ceiling level by running them through one horizontal course. There is no need to have two inclined shafts running through all the courses of the pyramid.

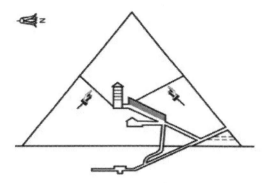

Orientation of the two channels in the "King's" Room

>>> Several photographs in support of the text of this chapter are to be found in the digital edition of this book as published in PDF and E-book formats.

CHAPTER 14.

KHAFRA'S PYRAMID

14.1 THE EXTERIOR

Next to Khufu **(Cheops)**'s Pyramid is Khafra (Chephren)'s Pyramid.

Khafra (Chephren), who succeeded Gedefra and reigned from 2520 to 2494 BCE, is credited with building this pyramid. Like all the other masonry pyramids, it is, essentially, anonymous.

The attribution to Khafra (Chephren) is made through Herodotus' account, and the surrounding funerary complex repeatedly makes reference to his name.

Δ Khafra's Pyramid
   Height: 471' (143.5 m)
   Base: 708' square (214.5 m)
   Mass: 5.3 million tons
   Inclination Angle: 53° 07' 48"

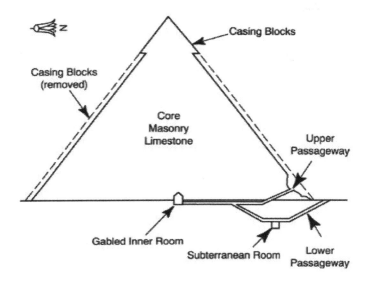

Even though this pyramid is slightly smaller than Khufu's Pyramid, it actually appears bigger than Khufu's because:1. It was built on a slightly higher ground than Khufu's.

2. It maintained its summit, while Khufu's pyramid lost its top 33' (10 m).

As it is the most preserved pyramid of the Giza group, it stands close to Khufu's, and, in size, is almost its twin.

An outcrop of local stone to the south and west of this pyramid is visible, since the original ground sloped, in this area. The Ancient Egyptians had to cut from two sides and fill the lower parts on the other two sides, in order to make the base absolutely level.

>> **This here is an important confirmation of the conditions of the local limestone—being very fragile and full of strata and fault lines. Just by looking at**

the perfect condition of the pyramid blocks and comparing them to the exposed natural rock onsite, it is easy to conclude that the blocks could never have come from local sources.

As another confirmation of the man-made stone of the pyramid blocks: just like Khufu's pyramid, the heights of the blocks here are staggered; but they all have the same width.

The uniform width of blocks is another indication that they were molded.

Also, Dr. Joseph Davidovits, the chemist and Egyptologist, checked the 22 steps near the top and found that they conform to 10 uniform lengths: yet more strong evidence of the use of standard molding forms. Even if, hypothetically, we ignore the dire conditions of the natural limestone, the blocks could never have been quarried with such uniform lengths.

As another confirmation of the man-made stone of the pyramid blocks, one can observe that, at some of these blocks, one can see the outline of a stone incorporated into the block, which means that such blocks were cast and could not have been quarried.

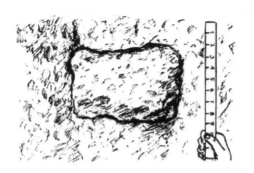

**A large rubble stone embedded
in a stone block**

Δ **The casing blocks here are distinguished by:**

– The upper courses consisting of fine-grained limestone casing blocks.
– The lower courses consist of granite casing blocks.
– The casing stones fit perfectly together, with
tongue and groove joints.
– There are still a large number of white limestone
casing stones, on the upper courses.
– There are no signs of a chipped corner at any of the
casting stones.

Δ Another confirmation of the man-made stone of the
pyramid blocks are the **huge paving blocks** around the
pyramids. One can clearly see these very durable, perfectly fitted, square-angled blocks. Each is several yards
(meters) in length.

They are joined together in such a beautiful strange mosaic.

Δ Similar patterns are also found by other pyramids and the causeways between each pyramid temple and its Valley Temple.

Δ Ancient Egyptians, throughout history, avoided simple abrupt interlocking joints. Creating uninterrupted continuous corners allowed the energies to flow unimpeded.

[For more information about the application of such intentional jointing pattern throughout the recovered history of Ancient Egypt, in temples, statues, walls, etc., refer to our book *The Ancient Egyptian Metaphysical Architecture* by Moustafa Gadalla.]

Δ   Δ   Δ

Δ The sacred geometry properties of this pyramid are found in its triangular cross-section. The pyramid of Khafra (Chephren) is basically twin 3:4:5 triangles, side-by-side, where the height would be 4 units to the base of 6.

More information was mentioned earlier, in chapter 6 of this book.

Δ   Δ   Δ

14.2 THE INTERIOR

The internal structure of this pyramid is of extreme simplicity in comparison to Khufu's pyramid.

There are two entrances, one directly above the other, leading into the pyramid. The upper entrance, 50′ (15 m) above ground, is the typical entrance, and the one which we use to enter.

The narrow passage follows the diagonal of a 1:2 rectangle, down into the bedrock. It levels off and then continues horizontally to a large limestone room. The walls of the sloping section and part of the horizontal section are lined with red granite, for unknown reasons. The passages are, again, totally devoid of any inscriptions.

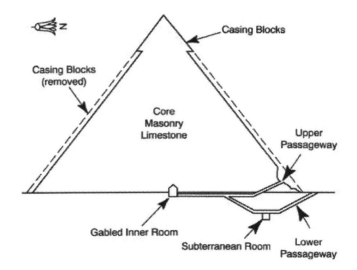

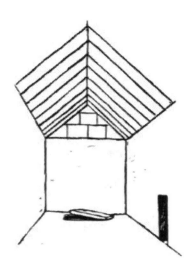

Khafra's Inner Room

The confined passage leads to the only room inside the pyramid. It is 46½' x 16½' x 22½' (14.2 m x 5 m x 6.9 m). This room is hewn out of the rock and roofed with gabled limestone slabs. These slabs are set at the same angle as the pyramid face.

This simple gabled roof is adequate to support the whole weight of the pyramid above it. Remember the roof of the "King's" Room in Khufu's pyramid? What they call the "relieving stones", above the "King's" Room, were not needed for structural purposes, because we can see here that a single gable above the flat ceiling would have sufficed, structurally.

So, what they termed as "relieving stones" in the "King's" Room of Khufu's Pyramid is not for structural purposes, but for other non-structural reasons

Δ This room was first found in 1818 by Belzoni. He

found that the entry close to the ground was plugged by 3 granite blocks.

Δ At the far western end of this totally bare room is an empty, uninscribed, beautiful, polished granite box 8.5' x 3.5' (2.6 m x 1.05 m) long and 3.3' (1.0 m) deep. This box is set into the floor of the room, up to the level of the lid.

Δ Belzoni found the lid broken into two pieces, nearby, when he first entered this pyramid in 1818. Belzoni never found a mummy or any sign of a funeral. There is no evidence whatsoever that Khafra or anyone else was ever buried in the stone chest which was embedded in the main room.

To reach the lower entrance of the pyramid, one must go outside the pyramid again, and look for the lower entrance.

Δ The lower passageway in the bedrock leads to a large, empty, uninscribed subterranean room.

Δ   Δ   Δ

>>> Several photographs in support of the text of this chapter are to be found in the digital edition of this book as published in PDF and E-book formats.

CHAPTER 15.

MENKAURA'S PYRAMID

The third pyramid of Giza is attributed to Menkaura (Mycerinus), who reigned from 2494 to 2472 BCE.

This pyramid, just like the other true-shaped pyramids, is anonymous. There are no inscriptions anywhere. Only the account of Herodotus, and references to his name in the surrounding mastabas, make him the likely builder.

This pyramid is much smaller than the other two pyramids of Khufu and Khafra. It is only 7% of the size of Khufu's pyramid, even though Menkaura reigned for 18 years and had plenty of time to build a pyramid as big as the other two pyramids of Giza.

>> Size was not his objective. These are not personal monuments. His pyramid is just a piece of the master plan, with its center at Saqqara. Yet, this small (and last) stone pyramid is the most harmonious of them all. It was the last of the series.

Δ   Δ   Δ

Looking again at the Giza Plateau:

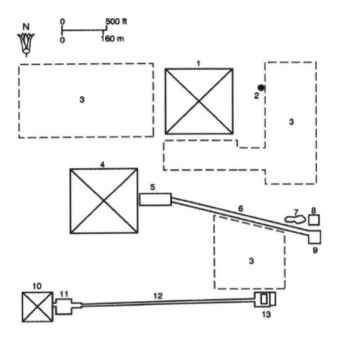

1. Great Pyramid of Khufu (Cheops).
2. Tomb of Hetepheres.
3. Mastaba Fields.
4. Pyramid of Khafra (Chephren).
5. Pyramid Temple of Khafra.
6. Causeway to Valley Temple of Khafra.
7. Great Sphinx.
8. Temple of the Sphinx.
9. Valley Temple of Khafra.
10. Pyramid of Menkaura (Mycerinus).
11. Pyramid Temple of Menkaura.
12. Menkaura Causeway.
13. Valley Temple of Menkaura.

15.1 THE EXTERIOR

The casing blocks here are different than the other two Giza pyramids. The lower half of the casing blocks are made of rough granite, except at the northern face of the pyramid, around the entrance, and in a corresponding area on the eastern face, where they are of fine granite.

The top half of the pyramid was fully dressed with fine-grained limestone, but the Arabs destroyed them. In 1196 CE, one of the Moslem rulers of Egypt tried to destroy this pyramid but had to stop because of the great expense.

Although it is the smallest and youngest of the three pyramids on the Giza Plateau, it has a very interesting harmonic design.

Δ Its cross section is very nearly an 5:8 triangle, representing the Neb (Golden) Proportion. Additionally, the ratio of the height to half the diagonal would be 8:9 (the perfect musical tone), with an angle between the edge and the horizontal of 51° 29' 53".

Δ Menkaura pyramid ends on a perfect or high note.

Δ   Δ   Δ

15.2 THE INTERIOR

The passageways here are very different from Khufu's and Khafra's.

There are two passageways:

1. The upper passageway has its entrance, as usual, on the northern face of the pyramid, and its entrance

is 13′ (4 m) above the base of the pyramid. This descending passage is the typical diagonal of a 1:2 rectangle, measuring about 102′ (31 m). The sloping section leads into a horizontal passage which, in turn, leads into the first inner room.

2. The second passageway is cut underneath the original upper passageway. The lower passageway is the one we use to enter the pyramid and it is lined with granite. It also, as usual, follows the slope of the diagonal of a 1:2 rectangle. The lower passage leads westward to a staircase, then down to a room containing six niches (called the Celled Room). Still further west lies the main underground room.

△ Cross section of Menkaura's Pyramid

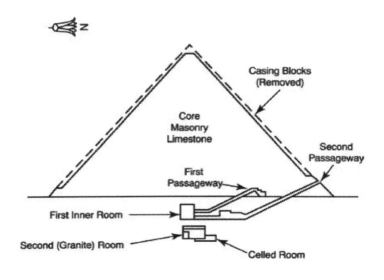

Base: 356′ square (108m)
Height: 218′ (67m)
Mass: 0.6 million tons

Slope: (face to base) 51° 20′ 25″ (5/4)
Slope: (edge to base) 51° 29′ 53″ (8/9)

The main underground room is cut out of bedrock; and again, it is entirely lined with red granite and totally devoid of any inscriptions. Its ceiling is a perfect barrel vault. The ceiling is formed of large, tightly fitted granite slabs. The undersides have been carved to provide the end supports for the vaulted ceiling.

This granite room, which is now empty, used to contain the only stone chest found in this pyramid. It is a basalt chest, with no inscriptions whatsoever. We hear that this stone chest was lost at sea when they tried to transport to Britain. Since it is "lost at sea", it was convenient to make up stories about it and pretend that it was the only missing evidence—which is out of our hands.

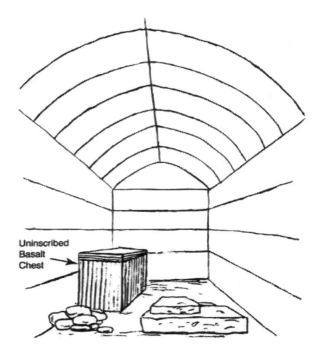

Main Underground Room in Menkaura's Pyramid

Δ This was the last TRUE pyramid of the Pyramid Age.

What a beautiful ending.

PART VII.

AFTER THE PYRAMIDS

CHAPTER 16.

MISSION ACCOMPLISHED

We subconsciously continue to think that the pyramids were personal monuments (which they were not). It is therefore that we have difficulty understanding why they stopped. They did not just stop. The job was completed.

The objective of building the pyramids as structures to attract and channel cosmic energy had been completed.

Δ   Δ   Δ

CHAPTER 17.

"PYRAMID" TEXTS

The earliest Egyptian funerary texts are found in the underground burial chamber and its ancillary rooms. It is these funerary texts, carved on the walls, that are called the "Pyramid Texts".

The "Pyramid Texts" are a collection of funerary literature that were found in tombs during the 5th and 6th dynasties (2465-2150).

The Egyptian masonry pyramids were built earlier, during the 4th dynasty. These pyramids are totally void of any inscriptions, as were shown throughout this book.

The true-shaped great pyramids of Giza, Dahshur, and Meidum were built during the 4th Dynasty (2575-2465 BCE), they have no inscriptions whatsoever, and in every other aspect, they differ from other earlier and later tombs simply because they are not tombs.

The most prominent place where these funerary texts are found is in the tomb of King Unas in Saqqara, at the end of the 5th dynasty (i.e. one hundred years after the last true-shaped solid masonry pyramid in the Giza Plateau was built).

These funerary texts are carved on the walls in the underground burial chamber and its ancillary rooms.

Δ　　　Δ　　　Δ

But if we look at the top of the Unas tomb, we find a pile of rubble. In this, like many cases we will show later, the Egyptians used the material that they excavated for the tomb, and simply placed this excess material on top of the tomb. They then built up a perimeter of solid stone around the heap of rubble in order to keep it in place.

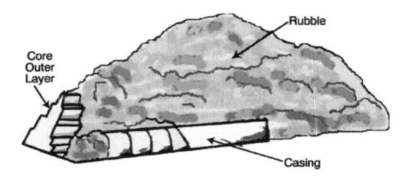

To call these heaps of rubble "pyramids" is intended to confuse the issue and mixes up the TRUE pyramids with tombs, to make them one and the same.

As such, calling certain Ancient Egyptian texts "Pyramid Texts" is a deceitful title, which is given by academia in order to shove it down our throats that the pyramids were tombs.

To untangle their web of deception, we must differentiate

between the masonry pyramids and the tombs that are covered by heaps of rubble. Only such tombs included these funerary texts.

These Texts form the basis for all subsequent funerary literature in Egypt, such as *The Book of the Coming Forth by Day* (known mistakenly as *The Book of the Dead*), *The Book of What is in the Duat* (or Underworld), *The Book of the Gates*, *The Book of Caverns*, *The Litany of Ra*, *The Book of Aker*, *The Book of Day*, and *The Book of Night*.

Such texts were not only for Kings, but the Texts were also inscribed in the coffins of the nobles and people of all classes.

The *Funerary* Texts help their souls to transform from their earthly existence to, as the Ancient Egyptian writings describe it:

> ...*"become a star of gold and join the company of Ra, and sail with him in his boat of millions of years."*

[For more information about Transformational ["funerary"] texts read *Egyptian Cosmology: The Animated Universe* by Moustafa Gadalla.]

Δ   Δ   Δ

>>> Several photographs in support of the text of this chapter are to be found in the digital edition of this book as published in PDF and E-book formats.

CHAPTER 18.

THE GREATEST PHARAOHS THAT FOLLOWED

There are those who baselessly claim that the extensive building during the Pyramid Age was a "public works project" to put people to work, and that the Egyptian economy "collapsed" afterwards as a result of such "excesses". Such notions are unfounded, outlandish, and contrary to recorded historical and archaeological facts.

In the Saqqara region, we find a simple tomb that was built by none other than King Pepi II (2246-2152 BCE). Yes, there is no dispute that he reigned for 94 years.

His burial chamber has a granite sarcophagus, which clearly identifies him as Pepi II.

Pepi II's tomb contains some fine hieroglyphs, but the superstructure is and was nothing more than a pile of rubble, like King Unas' structure. Pepi II was the fourth Pharaoh of the 6th Dynasty. He was very powerful and very rich and lasted long enough. His memorials are found throughout Egypt as well as various mines and quarries. He had the time and resources to build a pyramid like those in Giza, Dahshur, and Meidum, yet as shown above, he had but this one small, ungenuine *pyramid*..

Some other examples of royal tombs beneath heaps of rubble are also found in Dahshur next to the twin pyramids of Snefru—the Red and the Bent Pyramids.

There are ungenuine "pyramids" which belong to Amenemhet II (1929–1892 BCE), Sesostris III (1878–1844 BCE), and Amenemhet III (1844–1797 BCE). Each was made of a core of crude mud-brick, surrounded by an outer casing of limestone, now disappeared. Presently, they are just shapeless masses.

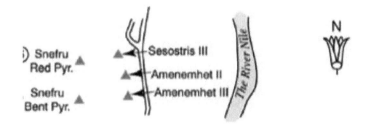

The economy flourished during their reigns, proving again that building masonry pyramids has nothing to do with the economy or with them being tombs.

Δ   Δ   Δ

>>> Several photographs in support of the text of this chapter are to be found in the digital edition of this book as published in PDF and E-book formats.

GLOSSARY

BCE – Before Common Era. Noted in many references as BC.

CE – Common Era. Noted in many references as AD.

Circle Index – designates the ratio of the circumference of a circle to its diameter, and is equal to 22/7.

concrete – a building material made of sand and gravel, bonded together with cement into a hard, compact substance.

cubit – The Ancient Egyptian unit of linear measurement, which is the distance between the elbow and the tip of the extended middle finger. One cubit = 1.72' (0.5236m).

Heb-Sed – an ancient festival associated with the rejuvenation and spiritual and physical renewal of the Pharaoh.

mastaba – means bench; a mud-brick, above-ground structure. The burial chambers of the deceased are found below the mastaba.

Neb (Golden) Proportion – is the "key to the structure of the cosmos". It is obtained using a rectangle of sides 1:2. If an approximation must be made, its value is 1.6180339.

Phi – (φ), see Neb (Golden) Proportion.

Pi – (π), see Circle Index.

pyramid – a solid figure having a polygonal base, the sides of which form the bases of triangular surfaces meeting at a common vertex.

"Pyramid" Texts – A collection of funerary literature that was found in the tombs of the Kings of the 5th and 6th Dynasties (2465–2150 BCE).

slope – the amount or degree of the deviation from the horizontal or vertical in an inclined surface: The ratio of the vertical difference divided by the horizontal difference.

SELECTED BIBLIOGRAPHY

Aldred, C. *Egypt to the End of the Old Kingdom*. London, 1965.

Alvarez, L. W. et al. *Search for Hidden Chambers in the Pyramids. Science* 167 (1970).

Badawy, Alexander. *Ancient Egyptian Architectural Design*. Los Angeles, CA, USA, 1965.

Badawy, A. 'The Stellar Destiny of Pharaoh and the so-called Air-shafts in Cheops's Pyramid', in *MIOAWB*, band 10, 1964.

Breasted, J. H. *History of Egypt*. Chicago, 1919.

Brecher, K. and Feirtag, M. *Astronomy of the Ancients*. Mass., 1979 ed.

Clarke, S. and Engelbach, R. *Ancient Egyptian Masonry*. Oxford, 1930.

Cornell, J. The First Stargazers, *An Introduction to the Origins of Astronomy*. London, 1981.

Davidovits, Dr. Joseph and Morris, Margie. *The Pyramids, An Enigma Solved*. New York, 1989.

De Cenival, Jean-Louis. *Living Architecture*. New York, 1964.

Edwards, I. E. S. *The Pyramids of Egypt. Rev. ed.* Harmondsworth, 1961; and London, 1972.

Erman, Adolf. *Life in Ancient Egypt.* New York, 1971.

Fakhry, Ahmed. *The Pyramids.* Chicago, 1969.

Firth, C. M., Quibell, J. E. and Lauer, J.-P. *The Step Pyramid. 2 vols.* Cairo, 1935-36.

Gadalla, Moustafa:
- *Ancient Egyptian Culture Revealed.* USA, 2007.
- *Egyptian Cosmology: The Animated Universe—2nd edition.* USA, 2001.
- *Egyptian Divinities: The All Who Are THE ONE.* USA, 2001.
- *Egyptian Harmony: The Visual Music.* USA, 2000.
- *Historical Deception: The Untold Story of Ancient Egypt.* USA, 1999.
- *Pyramid Handbook.* USA, 2000.

Gardner, Martin. *The Magic Numbers of Dr. Matrix.* New York, 1985.

Grinsell, L. *Egyptian Pyramids.* Gloucester, 1947.

Herodotus. *The Histories,* tr. A. de Selincourt. New York, 1954.

James, T. G. H. *An Introduction to Ancient Egypt.* London, 1979.

Lauer, J-P. *Le Probleme des Pyramides d' Egypte.* Paris, 1948.

Lemesurier, Peter. *The Great Pyramid Decoded.* New York, 1977.

Mendelssohn, Kurt. *The Riddle of the Pyramid.* New York, 1974.

Murray, Margaret A. *The Splendour that was Egypt.* New York, 1957.

Pennick, Nigel. *Sacred Geometry*. New York, 1982.

Petrie, W. M. F. *The Pyramids and Temples of Gizeh*. London, 1883.

Smyth, Piazza. *The Great Pyramid, Its Secrets and Mysteries Revealed*. London, 1880.

Stewart, Desmond. *The Pyramids and the Sphinx, Egypt Under the Pharaohs*. New York, 1977.

Tompkins, Peter. *Secrets of the Great Pyramid*. New York, 1971.

Trimble, V. '*Astronomical Investigations concerning the so called Air-shafts of Cheops's Pyramid*', in *JEA*, 21; 1936.

West, John Anthony. *The Travelers Key to Ancient Egypt*. New York, 1989.

Wilkinson, Sir J. Gardner. *The Ancient Egyptians, Their Life and Customs*. London, 1988.

Numerous references written in Arabic.

SOURCES AND NOTES

In my research, I came across dozens of books. Many of them are commercially oriented towards selling at any cost. I don't dignify such books by listing them, even though they sell very well.

Almost all my sources are written by very biased authors who (consciously or sub-consciously) have pro-Western and/or Judeo-Christian paradigms.

My references to the sources are listed in the previous section, Selected Bibliography. They are only referred to for the facts, events, and dates; not necessarily for their interpretations of such information.

It should be noted that if a reference is made to one of the author Moustafa Gadalla's books, that each of his books contains appendices for its own extensive bibliography as well as detailed Sources and Notes.

Chapter 2 (Genuine Pyr.)

> Primary Sources: Davidovits, Fakhry, Mendelssohn, Petrie, and West.
>
> Secondary Sources: All other listed references.

Chapter 3 (Saqqara.- Zoser)

Primary Sources: Badawy (Ancient Egyptian Architectural Design), Clarke, De Cenival, Edwards, Fakhry, Firth (Quibell and Lauer), Grinsell, James, Lauer, Mendelssohn, Pennick, and West.

Chapter 4 (Pyramids vs.Tombs)

Information on tombs, contents, and functions were obtained from: Erman, Gadalla, James, West, Wilkinson.

The difference between the Egyptian pyramids and tombs were obtained from Gadalla, Mendelssohn, and West.

Mendelssohn provided the most convincing points that destroy the academicians' "tomb theory". Other than that, the rest of the book is unfounded grandstanding and speculation.

Chapter 5 (Pyramid Complex)

Badawy (Ancient Egyptian Architectural Design), De Cenival, Gardner, Herodotus, Pennick, and West.

Chapter 6 (Pyramid Power)

Primary Sources: Gardner and West.

Abandonment

Primary Source: West

Secondary Sources: Practically all other listed references.

Chapter 7 & 8 (Construction Techniques)

The Common Theory

Practically all listed references.

Egyptian Know-How

Primary Sources: Davidovits, Firth (Quibell & Lauer), Gadalla (Historical Deception), West, and Wilkinson.

Secondary Sources: Other listed references.

Sources of stones

Primary Sources: Davidovits.

Davidovits, who is an expert in geopolymer and concrete technology, was very methodical in his presentation of facts related to the material and construction techniques. However, he was very careless in writing about historical and religious aspects of ancient Egypt. He did not hesitate to speculate in those areas without any evidence.

It should be noted that the author is a graduate civil engineer (1967) and has practiced civil engineering ever since. The author endorses Davidovits' findings in the areas of natural and manmade blocks, based on his knowledge of the technical subject matter and his numerous examinations of Egyptian monuments.

Synthetic and Natural Blocks

Primary Sources: Alvarez and Davidovits.

It should be noted that the author is a graduate civil engineer (1967) and has practiced civil engineering ever since. The author endorses Davidovits' findings in this particular area based on his knowledge of the technical subject matter and his numerous examinations of the Egyptian monuments.

Casing Stones

Primary Sources: Davidovits and West.

Secondary Sources: Practically all other listed references.

Fictional Ramps

Primary Sources: Davidovits and West.

Chapter 9 (Meidum)

Primary sources: Badawy (Ancient Egyptian Architectural Design), Davidovits, De Cenival, Fakhry, Lauer, Mendelssohn, Pennick, and West.

Secondary Sources: All other listed references.

Chapter 10 (Dahshur – Bent)

Primary Sources: Badawy (Ancient Egyptian Architectural Design), Davidovits, De Cenival, Fakhry, Lauer, Mendelssohn, Pennick, and West.

Secondary Sources: All other listed references.

Chapter 11 (Dahshur – Red)

Primary Sources: Badawy (Ancient Egyptian Architectural Design), Davidovits, De Cenival, Fakhry, Lauer, Mendelssohn, Pennick, and West.

Secondary Sources: All other listed references.

Chapter 12 (Giza Plateau)

Sources: Practically all listed sources.

Chapter 13 (Khufu)

Khufu – Exterior

Sources: Practically all listed sources.

For the harmonic proportion (sacred geometry) aspects: Badawy (Ancient Egyptian Architectural Design), De Cenival, Gardner, and West.

Khufu – Interior

Primary Sources: Smyth and West.

Secondary Sources: Practically all other listed references.

Chapter 14 (Khafra)

Khafra – Exterior

Configuration:

Primary: Davidovits, Fakhry, Lauer, and West.

Secondary: Practically all other listed references.

Construction: Davidovits (pyramid), West (paving blocks).

Harmonic Proportion (Sacred Geometry): Badawy (Ancient Egyptian Architectural Design)

Khafra – Interior

Primary Sources: Fakhry and West.

Secondary Sources: Practically all other listed references.

Chapter 15 (Menkaura)

Menkaura – Exterior

Configuration:

Primary: Davidovits, Fakhry, Lauer, and West.

Secondary: Practically all other listed references.

Construction: Davidovits (pyramid), West (paving blocks).

Harmonic Proportion (Sacred Geometry): Badawy (Ancient Egyptian Architectural Design)

Menkaura – Interior

Primary Sources: Fakhry and West.

Secondary Sources: Practically all other listed references.

Chapter 16 (Mission Accomplished)

Primary Sources: Davidovits and West.

Secondary Sources: Practically all other listed references.

Chapter 17 ("Pyramid" Texts)

Primary Sources: Practically all listed references

Chapter 18 (Pharaonic Tombs @ Saqqara & Dahshur)

Sources: Practically all listed sources.

TRF PUBLICATIONS

Tehuti Research Foundation (T.R.F.) is a non-profit, international organization, dedicated to Ancient Egyptian studies. Our books are engaging, factual, well researched, practical, interesting, and appealing to the general public. Visit our website at:

https://www.egypt-tehuti.org
E-mail address: info@egypt-tehuti.org

The publications listed below are authored by T.R.F. chairman,
Moustafa Gadalla.

The publications are divided into three categories:

[I] Current Publications in English Language
[II] Earlier Available Editions in English Language
[III] Current Translated Publications in Non English Languages[Chinese, Dutch, Egyptian(so-called "arabic"), French,German, Hindi, Italian, Japanese, Portuguese, Russian & Spanish]

[I] Current Publications in English Language

The Untainted Egyptian Origin—Why Ancient Egypt Matters

ISBN-13(pdf): 978-1-931446-50-1
ISBN-13(e-book): 9781931446-66-2

A short concise overview of some aspects of the Ancient Egyptian civilization that can serve us well nowadays in our daily life no matter where we are in this world.

The Ancient Egyptian Culture Revealed, Expanded 2ⁿᵈ ed.

ISBN-13(pdf): 978-1-931446-66-2
ISBN-13(e-book): 978-1-931446-65-5
ISBN-13(pbk.): 978-1-931446-67-9

Revealing several aspects, such as its remote antiquities, religious beliefs and practices; social/political system; buildings; language; music, comprehensive sciences; astronomy, medicine; economy; etc.

Isis : The Divine Female

ISBN-13(pdf): 978-1-931446-25-9
ISBN-13(e-book): 978-1-931446- 26-6
ISBN-13(pbk.): 978-1-931446-31-0

Explaining the metaphysical and physical divine female principle and about twenty female manifested attributes.

Egyptian Cosmology, The Animated Universe, Expanded 3ʳᵈ edition

ISBN-13(pdf): 978-1-931446-44-0
ISBN-13(e-book): 978-1-931446-46-4
ISBN-13(pbk.): 978-1-931446-48-8

Surveys the applicability of Egyptian cosmological concepts to our modern understanding of the nature of the universe, creation, science, and philosophy.

Egyptian Alphabetical Letters of Creation Cycle

ISBN-13(pdf): 978-1-931446-89-1
ISBN-13(e-book): 978-1-931446-88-4
ISBN-13(pbk.): 978-1-931446-87-7

The relationship between the sequence of the creation cycle and the Egyptian 28 ABGD alphabet.

Egyptian Mystics: Seekers of the Way, Expanded 2nd ed.

ISBN-13(pdf): 978-1-931446-53-2
ISBN-13(e-book): 978-1-931446-54-9
ISBN-13(pbk.): 978-1-931446-55-6

Egyptian alchemy and Sufism, with a coherent explanation of fundamentals and practices.

Egyptian Divinities: The All Who Are THE ONE, Expanded 2nd ed.

ISBN-13(pdf): 978-1-931446-57-0
ISBN-13(e-book): 978-1-931446-58-7
ISBN-13(pbk.): 978-1-931446-59-4

Details more than 80 Egyptian divinities (gods, goddesses) and their specific roles.

The Ancient Egyptian Roots of Christianity, *2nd ed.*

ISBN-13(pdf): 978-1-931446-75-4
ISBN-13(e-book): 978-1-931446-76-1
ISBN-13(pbk.): 978-1-931446-77-8

Egyptian roots of Christianity, both historically and spiritually.

The Ancient Egyptian Metaphysical Architecture, *Expanded Edition*

ISBN-13(pdf): 978-1-931446-63-1
ISBN-13(e-book): 978-1-931446-62-4
ISBN-13(pbk): 978-1-931446-61-7

Applications of sacred geometry, and number mysticism in Egyptian temples to generate cosmic energy.

Sacred Geometry and Numerology,

ISBN-13(e-book): 978-1-931446-23-5

This document is an introductory course for learning the fundamentals of sacred geometry and numerology, in its true and complete form, as practiced in the Egyptian traditions.

The Egyptian Hieroglyph Metaphysical Language

ISBN-13(pdf): 978-1-931446-95-2
ISBN-13(e-book): 978-1-931446-96-9
ISBN-13(pbk.): 978-1-931446-97-6

Scientific/metaphysical realities of pictorial images (Hieroglyphs) as the ultimate medium for the human consciousness that interpret, process and maintain the meanings of such images

---

The Ancient Egyptian Universal Writing Modes

ISBN-13(pdf): 978-1-931446-91-4
ISBN-13(e-book): 978-1-931446-92-1
ISBN-13(pbk.): 978-1-931446-93-8

The Egyptian Alphabetical language is the MOTHER and origin of all languages; and how it was diffused to become other 'languages' throughout the world.

The Enduring Ancient Egyptian Musical System—Theory and Practice, Expanded Second Edition

ISBN-13(pdf): 978-1-931446-69-3
ISBN-13(e-book): 978-1-931446-70-9
ISBN-13(pbk.): 978-1-931446-71-6

Fundamentals (theory and practice) of music, musical instruments, playing techniques, functions, etc.

Egyptian Musical Instruments, 2nd ed.

ISBN-13(pdf): 978-1-931446-47-1

ISBN-13(e-book): 978-1-931446-73-0
ISBN-13(pbk.): 978-1-931446-74-7

This book presents the major Ancient Egyptian musical instruments, their ranges, and playing techniques.

The Musical Aspects of the Ancient Egyptian Vocalic Language

ISBN-13(pdf): 978-1-931446-83-9
ISBN-13(e-book): 978-1-931446-84-6
ISBN-13(pbk.): 978-1-931446-85-3

Shows that the fundamentals, structure, formations, grammar, and syntax are exactly the same in music and in the Egyptian alphabetical language.

Egyptian Romany: The Essence of Hispania, *Expanded 2nd ed.*

ISBN-13(pdf.): 978-1-931446-43-3
ISBN-13(e-book): 978-1-931446- 90-7
ISBN-13(pbk.): 978-1-931446-94-5

Shows the intimate relationship between Egypt and Hispania archeologically, historically, culturally, ethnologically, linguistically, etc.

Made in the USA
Columbia, SC
19 October 2018